I0529774

TRUSTING THE ENEMY
Letters from the Past
Book 2

TINA CLOUGH

TRUSTING THE ENEMY

Copyright © Tina Clough 2022

The author asserts her moral right to be identified as the author of this work.

PAPERBACK ISBN 978-1-99-118711-6

Lightpool Publishing

www.lightpoolpublishing.com

Cover and book design by Andrene Low

Chapter 1

On a sunny August Saturday at the Okehampton Castle ruins, for the second time in her life, Callista feels someone else's thoughts invade her mind, and she stumbles and nearly falls. She feels dizzy and clutches her head as her vision blurs, external noises momentarily distant and muted.

A couple walking behind her run forwards and appear one on each side of her, the woman reaches out and takes hold of her arm to steady her.

'Are you all right? Are you feeling ill?'

Callista shakes her head and tries to pull her thoughts together, as the pain in her head recedes. 'No, no - I'm fine, but that man has a gun!'

She takes a deep breath to compose herself, her focus returns and suddenly she feels intensely energized and determined.

The husband stares at her, his thin face creased with concern. 'Which man? The one down there? Why do you think he has a gun?'

His sounds calm and Callista swings around to look at him, shakes his wife's hand off her arm and says urgently. 'Yes, he does – I think he's going to shoot those children!'

She points towards the parking area at the bottom of the hill where a woman is mustering a small group of children ahead of her to climb the slope up to the castle ruins.

'No, no, you're just confused,' says the woman, comforting and kind. 'Don't worry, dear – I'm sure he hasn't got a gun.'

Two young men have joined them now, the mention of a gun has caught their attention and Callista is certain that she has only moments to act and turns to the newcomers, frantic, begging. 'Help me, please! We must stop him – he has a gun!'

Her four companions look at each other and then back at her, nobody moves and inside her mind the urgency mounts to a crescendo and she knows, without knowing how, that there is no time left to talk, it will happen any second now. The children have started up the slope, laughing and talking, their shrill voices like a flock of distant birds.

She sprints forward faster than she has ever run in her life and sees the man's right arm bend as he reaches in under his jacket. She launches herself at him in a flying side-on tackle and her shoulder slams into his back. He falls to his knees with her tumbling half over him and then rolling down to one side.

The young men are there in seconds and the scene turns instantly chaotic. The man has a gun in his hand and is trying to get to his feet, but one of the others grabs his free hand and wrenches the gunman's arm back and up behind him, and he turns his head and looks straight at Callista. She has time to think how utterly normal he looks before she notices that his hand with the gun has swung towards her. Instinctively she rolls away from him instead of trying to get up and a moment later the other young man throws himself down between her and the gun man, pushing her further away as he lands. The gun goes off and everything seems to stop; for a moment she hears nothing but the sound of the heavy breathing of the struggling men.

She gets to her feet, vaguely aware that people are running towards them, shouting. In front of her both young men are lying across the gun man holding him down, and he still has the gun in his outstretched hand. He twists under the weight on his back and struggles to throw them off, and every time he twists the gun moves, points in another direction. It might go off again any second, and someone might be shot; she takes three short steps forward and kicks his hand hard and the

3

gun flies in an arc through the air and lands further down on the grass slope. People are closing in now, clustering undecided around the struggling men, uncertain of what to do to help. Further down the slope a woman runs forward and bends to pick up the gun. An older man lowers himself ponderously to kneel on the legs of the gun man and anchors him to the ground. One of the young men turns his head and says, panting, 'Has anyone got a belt - or something to tie him with?'

Tying him is a chaotic process, with people shouting instructions at each other as they hold him down, but after a frantic struggle his hands and feet are bound with the help of a man's belt and a long scarf. After screaming and struggling throughout the process of being tied, the gun man suddenly goes quiet and lies still, his face turned to one side; he looks vaguely surprised but no longer aggressive. The young men get up and stand one each side of him staring at each other across his body, hot and panting, they look as if they are only just realising what they have done, and a man from the crowd helps the old man up.

Callista takes in the scene with a feeling of strangely detached interest, glances down the grass slope and sees the children clustered around a woman and slips sideways through the crowd, her only thought now is to avoid having to talk to anyone. The husband of the couple, who spoke to her earlier, is talking on his

4

phone with one arm around his wife's shoulders, people are asking each what happened and taking photos. Everyone's attention is on the bound man on the ground, and nobody notices her leave. The burst of energy and the feeling of being able to do anything at all is over and now she feels exhausted, ready to lie down on the ground and go to sleep. She walks further away from the excited crowd and sits down on a block of fallen masonry from the ruins, leans back against a taller stone and closes her eyes; she knows she should leave now, go down to the car park and disappear, but she needs to sit for a moment first, to gather her thoughts and try to understand what just happened.

Someone sits down beside her; she opens her eyes and sees the woman who first talked to her. 'My dear,' she says. 'That was very brave! I'm so sorry we didn't believe you. Are you hurt?'

'No, I'm fine – I think it's just shock, I just need to collect myself a bit.'

'What a blessing that shot didn't hit anyone – when the gun went off, I really worried it would have hit you, but the bullet must have just disappeared over the top of the hill. Nobody seems to be hurt. What a dreadful thing to happen in a place like this with so many people around!'

Her husband leaves the group of people he has been talking to and joins them, still with his phone in his hand.

'That was a marvellous tackle!' he says approvingly, as if he is her rugby coach. 'You had him on his knees in one move - and a fine sprint! Well done!' Then he crouches down in front of her and looks closely at her. 'Are you all right? You look a bit pale.'

Callista brushes her hair away from her face and tries to smile. 'Just reaction, I think – there's nothing wrong with me.'

The man rises to his feet and stands looking down at her with a frown. 'But now you must tell us, how did you know he had a gun? Do you know him? Had you followed him?'

'God, no! I've never seen him before – I have no idea who he is. I was walking away from the ruins to get a bit further out on the hill, just looking at the view and I noticed him a few yards in front of me. He stood there without moving and I just felt...' She stops and they both stare at her.

'What did you feel? Did he say something? I can't understand how you knew!'

She knows it's pointless trying to explain, it's too complicated and confusing, and her best option is to sound innocently muddled and avoid any mention of what went on in her head the moments before they stopped to ask if she was ill.

'I don't know,' she says slowly. 'I can't explain it. No, I didn't see a gun and he hadn't said anything – it was just a feeling I had. I felt panic-stricken, terrified –

and I saw those children down there and I could tell that he was looking straight at them.'

The wife gets to her feet and the two of them stand side by side looking down at her, and their faces reflect their feelings: fascination, confusion and disbelief.

I must get away from here, thinks Callista, this could turn into a circus, and any minute now the police will arrive and then I'll have to make some kind of statement, and it will take forever. And they will ask me to explain – which I can't. I must get away from all these people!

'Excuse me, please,' she says. 'I feel a bit funny – I think I'd better get down to the toilets in the parking area right away!'

Without waiting for their reaction, she gets up and walks quickly back towards the ruins instead of taking the shortcut down the grass slope, which would involve walking past the ever-growing crowd around the gun man, who still lies on the ground. She jogs through the open area surrounded by remnants of the old castle and continues down the wide path towards her car. People coming up from the parking area have no idea what has just happened and stare at her hurrying past them, but she doesn't notice; her entire focus is on getting to her car and leaving this place behind.

She thinks she has escaped notice, but just as she unlocks the door of her car a voice calls out behind her. 'Hey, don't go - wait a moment!'

One of the young guys, who wrestled the gun man to the ground, has followed her and slows to a walk when he sees that she has noticed him. He starts talking excitedly long before he reaches her. 'That was brilliant, what you did! Super cool! Are you OK?'

She stares at him for a moment, at a loss about what to say and opens the car door. 'I'm fine, thank you! You and your friend were pretty cool too. And it was you who threw yourself towards me and pushed me away, wasn't it?'

'Yeah, I thought he was going to shoot you, I could see him moving the gun towards you.'

'I think maybe you saved my life' she says, itching to get away, but wanting to give him credit and to let him know that she appreciates what he did. 'It was good teamwork – I'm really glad you and your mate were there!'

He comes closer as she speaks and she knows he wants her to stay, to talk through it and maybe explain how this happened so suddenly, but she cannot abide any further conversation.

She gets into the car and swings out of her parking space, glances in the rear vision mirror as she drives away and sees the phone in his raised hand; he is taking a photo of her leaving. Driving back to Exeter takes all her concentration. She tries to dismiss any thoughts of what just happened and focuses on driving safely, but in the back of her mind images pop up, like snapshots both of the event she has just experienced and of the one nearly exactly a year ago in Salcombe. She turns on the radio, hoping to distract her mind, but despite her efforts to keep them at bay, fragments of visual memory insert themselves into her consciousness; the man's elbow bending as he reached inside his jacket to pull out the gun, seeing the gun still in his hand pointing straight at her, the scream of tyres as a car accelerated towards her, the cacophony of breaking glass and metal ripping apart, the look on the girl's face as they lay on the pavement, the gun flying through the air like a black bird, the face of the gunman. Images from a year ago and from today change places and move past each other like the glass pieces inside a kaleidoscope - a constantly changing pattern that she cannot ignore however hard she tries.

When she climbs the stairs to the flat, she feels exhausted, both mentally and physically. There is a note from Becks on the kitchen bench: Gone to Torquay for long lunch with Karen, Simon et al. Might continue to Simon's cottage, prob not home until late or tomorrow.

Callista stands there in the late afternoon sun, unable to decide if she is disappointed that Becks has gone out, most likely for the night, or relieved that she isn't home and there is no need to talk about what happened. Briefly, but only very briefly, she contemplates calling her mother, but the ramifications are hard to predict, and she decides not to. Accepting one strange event as a random, unexplained phenomenon, is one thing; asking her mother to not worry about a second, and very similar, event is too much to ask. Better to leave it until tomorrow or the next day and get some space to think through it by herself.

By evening she feels on an even keel again and makes comfort food for dinner. With a bowl of macaroni cheese and a glass of red wine she curls up on the sofa to watch a soppy movie on Netflix, but every now and again the recurring thought occurs: will this terrifying phenomenon eventually take over her mind, or is it over now, was this the last time?

Chapter 2

What a blessing, thinks Callista when she gets out of the shower and dries herself off before rubbing her long hair dry with the towel. This is the first Sunday for ages that I've had the flat to myself after months of tripping over Becks' boyfriend every Sunday morning. I hope she really has ditched him – she needs to find someone she can get serious about, someone who will last. I've never understood why she keeps hooking up with guys far less clever than she is herself. Sometimes I wonder what they think when they gradually discover what sits behind that cute exterior – do they feel intimidated? She's got a mind like a steel trap when she lets you see it, and she can out-reason most people. Scenes of political debate from the school staff room pop into her mind and makes her smile into the mirror.

She slips into her kimono and is tying the belt when the doorbell rings. If it isn't boyfriends slumped on the sofa watching sport on a Sunday morning, it's not being able to mooch around in a kimono, she thinks as she walks to the door. I hope it's not somebody who wants to come in, I need some time to myself.

'Callista Bannister?' asks the middle-aged policewoman on the doorstep. 'I'm Constable Yung, Mary Yung. Have you got time to talk to me for a few minutes? It's about the incident at Okehampton Castle yesterday.'

Here it comes, thinks Callista. Somehow, they found me, and now I'll have to play this down as much as I can. She shows Constable Yung into the living room and offers her a cup of tea. 'No, it's no trouble – I've just come out of the shower, and I was heading for the kitchen to make tea anyway, would you like a cup?'

'Now then, Callista,' says Mary Yung when they have their mugs of tea. 'Call me Mary! And if you ever need me, my surname is pronounced 'young' but it's spelled without the o. Yesterday you were at the Okehampton Castle ruins and you alerted others to the fact that a man close by was armed and potentially dangerous. You tackled him before some bystanders helped to subdue him. Is that right?'

'Yes, that's right.' Volunteer nothing, she thinks, the less we delve into this mystery, whatever it is, the better.

How can I explain it to others when I don't understand it myself?

'We have talked to one of the people who called the police, a man who says you spoke to him and his wife shortly before this happened. You told them the man had a gun, but they thought you were mistaken.' She stops talking and looks a question at Callista, leaving her no choice but to respond.

'Yes, I thought he had a gun.'

'Do you know him?'

'No.

'Had you spoken to him – had he told you he had a gun, or had you seen the gun?'

'No.'

Mary Yung tilts her head to one side with a slight frown. 'So why did you say, "that man has a gun and he's going to shoot those children". Where did that suspicion come from? What was it that alerted you?'

Callista sits silent, turns the mug around and around and tries to imagine what she can say and can't think of anything that would make sense.

'There's no need to worry - we're not suspecting you of being involved. And we have plenty of witness statements about his behaviour earlier on - we wondered if you had perhaps noticed him earlier, perhaps in the carpark, seen the gun inside his open jacket perhaps? Or overheard him talking to himself.' She smiles. 'He had been talking to himself quite a bit

– several witnesses mentioned it. Perhaps you heard him say something as you approached him?'

'I don't think I can have heard him– he had his back to me, and he was a little way in front of me, but I can't be sure. I had just got there, I walked up the regular path, not up the grass slope. I can't recall seeing him at all before that very moment.'

She knows that saying she had heard him say something will solve one of her problems, but it might just add a new one. If witnesses have mentioned how far behind him she was, it will be obvious that she can't have heard anything, even if he was talking to himself, because he was too far in front of her. And if she had come close to him earlier, how would she explain not having alerted anyone else to the fact that there was a man muttering to himself about having a gun and planning to kill people?

Mary Yung studies her face while these thoughts swirl through Callista's head and now she smiles. 'Well, let's leave that to one side for now. You were caught by three cameras that were already filming the views, and someone took a photo of your car when you drove out of the parking area, so that's how we found you. You've not been online this morning?'

'Oh, no – don't tell me it's online!' That she had not checked this already seems very odd now; there is always someone walking around with a phone in their hand these days, ready to press the button and start

14

filming. It makes her cringe to think of video and photos all over the internet. She sighs, defeated. 'OK, I'll tell you what I know, but I can guarantee that you won't believe me – I don't believe it myself.'

'Do you mind if I record it?' asks Mary Yung and gets her phone out. 'If it's complicated it might be easier for me than trying to make notes. And this is very informal, it's not an interview as such, so you can say whatever you want to.'

Callista collects her thoughts, makes a rapid evaluation of whether to include the first incident a year ago and decides not to. The last thing she wants is for this to become more sensational than it already is. A strange and seemingly impossible thing might happen to somebody once, by chance and randomly; twice would be alarming and indicate a pattern and cause a lot of interest.

'I was walking a short distance down the slope just looking at the view - and I was just about to turn around to take a photo of the ruins outlined against the sky. The man was about ten meters in front of me, moving slowly forward and then suddenly he stopped and stood still, looking down to the left. And I had this crazy thought that he had gun, that he was going to do something dreadful - and *then* I noticed that what he was looking at was a little group of children starting up the hill towards us.'

Yung waits for a moment and then she says, 'Yes?

15

Was that when that couple came up to you? They say you stumbled and clutched your head - they thought you were ill.'

'They didn't believe me, of course – well, who would? It must have sounded completely mad - all I could tell them was that I thought he had a gun and that he was thinking of shooting the children. I still can't explain it and it's driving me crazy!'

She can hear how tense her voice is, and she sees the speculation in Young's eyes. 'I know what you're going to say – and believe me, I've said it to myself a hundred times since yesterday - I hardly got any sleep. Why did I think he had a gun under his jacket? How could I be so sure of it that I tackled him like that? I was totally certain I had to do something immediately to prevent a tragedy – there was not the slightest doubt in my mind. And if it hadn't been for those two young guys it could have gone terribly wrong - he could have shot those children even from that kneeling position after I tackled him. And there's no way I could have kicked the gun out of his hand, if those guys hadn't thrown themselves on top of him, kind of holding him down.'

Mary Yung nods. 'We have found out more about him, of course - he is very unwell, mentally unwell right now. He suffers from paranoid schizophrenia, which is supposed to be managed by medication, but it seems he might have stopped taking his meds. The halfway house where he's been living doesn't have live-in staff, he is expected to take his drugs without supervision.'

'But the gun! How did he get a gun? Surely someone with a mental disorder can't go out and buy a gun? It seems mad!'

'We don't know where he got the gun from – there's no way he could get it through ordinary channels, but he's not saying much that makes sense at the moment. He told the arresting officer that he had received a confidential message telling him that he must prove his loyalty by killing someone – a voice had told him. It's the kind of episode that can happen with this disease if the medication stops working or if they don't take it.'

They sit in silence for a moment, then Mary Yung lifts her mug of tea and salutes Callista. 'Amazing! Totally amazing! You can't explain it, and neither can I, but be prepared for the press to track you down – because it's only a matter of time. Those videos are on all social media, they'll be global and viral by tonight. And they're very good too, especially the one that's the longest and proving the most popular – the guy who held that phone must have just stood there steady as a rock holding the phone focused on the scene. And it was the best angle to get it all – a bit to one side of you and higher up. He got the whole thing, from the first stumble when you clutch your head to the sprint and the tackle – and then your kick that sent the gun flying, amazing!'

'Why did you come? Was it just to make sure I didn't know him?' asks Callista when they stand in the hall. 'You don't seem to have suspected I was involved, even when you first came - though I noticed that you asked questions before you told me there was video of it.'

Because, she thinks, if they were lucky, as they were, and I hadn't yet known about the video, I might have told a different story - if I was a liar. Isn't that what they do, to see if you're trying to hide something?

'Oh no, not at all – the evidence that couple gave us was pretty graphic. I was just asked to go and check you're all right and to see if you could explain what happened and to check if you want some support - if you're traumatized you can have counselling, we'll organise it. Sorry, I should have mentioned this earlier. It's been interesting to read what's been found out so far and I thought you'd like to know. That couple who first approached you – they said it was obvious you were in some kind of very sudden trouble; perhaps intense pain and they couldn't stop saying how sorry they were that they didn't believe you. They are full of admiration for your courage.'

'I know – they came and talked to me afterwards when I was sitting on one of the stone blocks. I think they were as shocked as I was. I don't know if maybe they can vouch for it that I never was anywhere near that man before it happened.'

'Don't worry about that – a family of five, who were right behind you as you walked up from the parking area, saw you walk through the ruins and out onto the grass – and that man was already out there, standing a bit higher up on the hillside at first, so clearly you hadn't heard him talking or seen the gun earlier on. You arrived behind him just as he started walking forward slowly. He had arrived by car about an hour before you and just walked around – people said he kept staring at them and mumbling to himself. I suppose it's a lucky thing that he didn't shoot anyone before you put him out of action. And I must add that everyone we interviewed was very intrigued by your reaction – and so am I, more than ever after talking to you! So be prepared for the media storm, they'll be on to this in no time. Here's my card, please get in touch if you need me.'

Chapter 3

I wish I could be as enthusiastic as she is, thinks Callista as she closes the door behind Constable Yung, but I can't - this situation fills me with dread. It might turn into a nightmare, and I'll become known as that freak who thinks she has extrasensory powers, which is the last thing I want to be, particularly as I don't believe in all that semi-mystical stuff. Such an oxymoron to have something like this happen, and to know that it really did happen, and at the same time I can honestly say that I don't believe this sort of thing is real. And I have no explanation at all, don't understand how it happened or what caused it.

Getting dressed can wait, she must first check what's on the internet and start making plans for how to deal with the fallout, because there's no doubt in her mind that there will be fallout. The way Mary Yung described what she had already seen made it sound like just the sort of thing that would go viral nearly instantly. Finding the video on social media takes seconds, it is spreading fast and a still photo of her tackling the gun man is on two of the newspaper websites as is one of her kicking the gun out of his hand. Feeling uneasy about how fast this is developing she goes to make breakfast but doing something practical doesn't divert her mind from thinking and planning.

With another mug of tea and a piece of toast beside her, she studies the video, plays it over and over and stares at herself stumbling and bending forward, hands to her temples. She tries to recapture what her senses were telling her at that precise moment. Tries to conjure up additional detail, maybe her mind will reveal some little thing she has forgotten, something that might make sense of it all.

The video is taken from up at the castle ruins and shows a wide sweep of green countryside with low rolling hills and the roofs of houses in Okehampton village beyond clumps of trees. Someone stood on one of the higher walls, she thinks and takes an absent-minded sip of tea, and they were just filming the view, doing a slow sweep across the landscape and then they caught the exact moment when I stopped and sort of stumbled, and they kept filming what was happening.

Now that the video is out there, people will ask me

about it and I will have nothing to say, apart from 'I don't know how it works' and 'yes, it happened, but I have no extra-sensory powers'. And then what will happen? They'll just keep on nagging me, so I'd better practice a few phrases and make sure it sounds right when I say them, so I can just trot them out when I need them. And I'd better let Mum and Dad know in case someone comes knocking on their door. I'm glad tomorrow is a Bank Holiday, so I don't have to go back to school until Tuesday. And I do hope there isn't anything from Salcombe waiting to leap out at me. Maybe someone, who saw it or filmed it, will recognize me on the Okehampton video and then it will be impossible to deny that this is crazy thing has happened to me twice. But were there any shots in the caste ruin video where my face shows clearly enough for someone who doesn't know me, to recognize me?

She starts the video again; she watches her hands go to her head and how she stands slightly stooped with her hands over her temples and the couple come rushing up to her. I do look as if I'm having an attack of some sort – and that's what it felt like, an attack on my mind. But it's filmed from an angle, my face doesn't show. Now the woman is talking to me and I've lifted my head, and there is the point when the man dismisses what I'm saying, and those younger guys stop to listen, I bet they heard me mention the gun. Oh no, there it is – where I swing around and tell those two guys that we

22

must do something – full face towards the camera, damn it!

The sight of how she sprinted forward from a standing start, hurtling herself into the back of the man with the gun surprises her every time she watches it. My God! I had no idea I could run that fast, and that flying tackle! If someone had told me I could do that, I would never have believed it, quite impressive. And the way the man falls forward onto his knees and I roll off him to the side – it's like something choreographed for a scene in a film, it looks too good to be an impromptu action, but it's just how it happened.

She studies the boys struggling with the gun man and thinks, there's no doubt I might have been the first victim if they hadn't done what they did, particularly the one who flung himself between me and the gun man. Look at him, he's turns his head my way and his hand with the gun moves and now it's aimed right at me, and then that boy kind of rolls back towards him and gets to his feet and throws himself over the man's back. God, we were all so lucky! But I didn't realise how fast it all happened, from the time I tackle the man to the point where I get to my feet, take a few steps closer and kick his hand. Literally just seconds. And look at the gun flying through the air, amazing luck really. It might have gone off again instead of being disposed of harmlessly, but I didn't think of that at the time, that I could have caused someone to be shot. But at least it was out of reach after that. And there's that woman running forward to pick it up, thank God someone did. What an incredible piece of video, no wonder it's going viral, it *is* like an action sequence in a film. Now I'm going to work out exactly what I'm going to say to people, before I do anything else, there's no way I can stay anonymous – everyone who knows me will recognize me and they'll put my name in comments and share it, they won't be able to resist. And that means that if anything is going to surface about the Salcombe incident, it won't be long before it appears.

She looks absentmindedly at her empty hand; she has eaten her toast without even noticing. However many times she turns the problem over in her mind, she comes up with no way of explaining away what happened. There is nothing she can say, apart from that she doesn't know how it happened. She can't deny that something happened; the video shows clearly that something was going on and that it affected her badly, a physical reaction. She can't deny that the certainty that something would happen was so compulsive, so overwhelming, that she felt that her only option was to tackle the man by herself - her actions prove it.

She will just say exactly what she said to Mary Yung, that she doesn't understand it and can't explain it. But she is glad Mary came, or she would not have known that there is genuine proof she was never anywhere near the gunman until the very moment her mind warned her something was going to happen. Now Callista can quote her, and nobody can try to imply she was involved in any way.

When she turns her phone on, it emits a seemingly endless stream of beeps from social media alerts and emails, but she ignores them. The most important thing now is to call her parents and warn them.

'No, there's nothing you can do. I just wanted to warn you because it's going viral,' says Callista to her parents on Skype. 'It's probably the sort of thing that the media love – makes it easy for them to get people interested and with that video already out there it's perfect for them. It feeds into that brand of rubbish I always think of as "magic crystal beliefs" - people will love it.'

'You're quite right, it's taken off already,' says her father. 'I haven't told Liz, but I've seen the video on social media multiple times, I spotted it just half an hour ago and everyone I know is sharing it and commenting on it. I've had three of our friends already sending private messages from Facebook, asking if you're all right. And it's on YouTube too – I checked just now, and it has been watched nearly a million times and I'm not surprised. It's very dramatic, darling, but it does worry me a little that you felt you should tackle someone holding a gun. But to go back to how it happened – please tell me again what it was you thought was happening inside your head. What did you think it was – someone telling you something, like a warning. Or reading someone else's mind?'

'For God's sake! Don't answer him,' says her mother crossly. 'I *cannot* believe he didn't tell me right away when he first saw this! Fancy not telling me about a thing like that happening to you – Callista, you father is very odd sometimes! I'll go and look at it as soon as we finish talking. You can tell us more later, there's no need to upset yourself further right now. And don't worry about the press – if they come here, we can deal with it. We just have to prepare what we'll say, so we are ready if they do.'

Amazing, she thinks, this is so typical, and it would be quite funny if it were about somebody else. Dad is just mildly concerned but mostly curious. Empathy isn't his strong suit, he might be on the Aspberger's spectrum – he is definitely a bit odd, as Mum always says, not that she seems to mind, and neither do I really. And Mum will remember the incident in Salcombe and hope that it won't be brought into this, just like I do, so she's a bit worried.

'I'm sure it will get worse,' she says now and smiles at her parents, who have watched her thinking, and probably wondered what was going on in her head. 'So, you're right, Mum - you'd better be prepared for when the press finds you. These days people can find out everything without ever having set eyes on you. And people who know me will tell others. So, decide now what you're going to say, if some reporter comes knocking on your door. And Mum – please don't talk to anyone about what happened in Salcombe.'

'I have no memory of anything happening,' says her mother with a straight face. 'I can't even remember going to Salcombe with you. Are you sure you're not confusing me with someone else?'

Callista grins. 'You're the best! Goodbye both of you, I must go and get dressed before Becks returns and finds me in my kimono at lunch time!'

She mutes her phone and puts it face down on the table. The last thing she needs now is to be forced to discuss this again.

Chapter 4

The loud shout from the sitting room makes Callista jump where she is standing by the kitchen bench, contemplating the dinner ingredients she just got out of the fridge.

'Come here - quick, quick!' yells Becks from the sitting room. 'You're on the news, girl!' And a second later she yells, 'Wow! Awesome tackle! Go girl!'

Standing in the kitchen doorway she watches Becks watching the video clip that she herself has already seen a dozen times. Becks' eyes are glued to the screen, she is leaning forward, completely absorbed in what she is seeing.

'Shit, Callista,' she says when the video is over, and the news moves on to the next topic. 'They played it twice! Why didn't you tell me about this? I had no idea this had happened. Come over here and sit down – this is riveting, I want to hear all about it.'

'How could I tell you? You just came in ten minute ago after being out since before lunch yesterday – you made it home just in time to turn on the evening news. Which you did. And where was I and what was I doing? I was in the kitchen making our dinner! There hasn't been time to tell you, but I was going to – over dinner. You must be the last person in the country to hear about it – it's gone viral, it's literally everywhere. How come you didn't see it already? Your phone is never out of your hand. And why is it that suddenly your vocab has changed to something that reminds me of an American teenage show,' asks Callista, irritated at her friend's unholy enjoyment of what is for her a traumatic memory.

'Are we feeling a bit grumpy today?' says Becks, not in the least put out by Callista's irritation. 'Did things not work out so well this weekend?'

'I have no idea what you are talking about. The only plans I had for the long weekend was that damned excursion yesterday – on my own – to Okehampton to check out the ruins. I read a really interesting thing online about the history of the castle and thought I'd go and have a look. I've never been there, and we've lived here for three years.'

'Sad, sad, sad,' says Becks and gets up. 'Since you ditched that fiancé of yours, you've not had quite so

29

much fun, have you? I'll pour you some of this New Zealand Sauvignon Blanc that Shane recommended – I put it in the fridge yesterday morning, it's gorgeous. You need cheering up, this thing hasn't put you in a good mood, has it?'

I'm half in inch from screaming at her, thinks Callista, when Becks goes to the kitchen. She always refers to Harry as 'that fiancé of yours' – just because she never liked him. But she was right, of course, he is what someone in the old days would have called a scoundrel, no, he is worse – he is a manipulator. Handsome and sexy and always keen to have fun, but bad all the same. And Becks knew it from the start, but I was infatuated and wouldn't listen. And she is right – I haven't been out a lot lately, but I don't mind half as much as she thinks I ought to.

Becks returns carrying the bottle of wine, her phone with the charger attached and dangling, and two glasses suspended upside down between her fingers. 'Here it is – can you take the bottle out of my hand please?'

She puts the glasses on the table in front of the sofa and bends to plug the charger in beside the TV, and Callista says, 'Did you wear those stretch jogging pants all the time you were out? If you did, I hope you didn't bend over the way you did just now in front of anyone you don't trust to behave – being blond and cute isn't an excuse for being careless. I could see every detail of your genital anatomy.'

'Really?' Becks laughs. 'What a cheap thrill for the rest of the world. But I must tell you why I've been cut off from the news and the media - I left my phone in my car, on the dashboard, in the sun, for six hours yesterday when we were in Torquay! It hasn't worked since, and someone told me to put it in the freezer overnight and then try to charge it. I'll try it now, but it's probably dead.'

She fills the glasses and sits down, pats Callista's leg and smiles. 'Tell me! The commentary on the news was minimal, but intriguing.'

At the end of the recital, Becks frowns and now she is serious. 'This is *not* good! I think you are right about this having the potential to become very tiresome. It's got all the main ingredients of a great media storm – a young, and may I say it, gorgeous woman, a homicidal man with a gun, cute little innocent kids– not that we know they were cute, but kids are always referred to as cute when they're in the news - and a mystical ESP type connection. Not to mention ancient castle ruins - it's the perfect package. Before we know it, somebody will invent an Okehampton Curse and claim you're a victim of it.'

She drinks some wine and looks hard at Callista. 'So, there will be trouble - there will be headlines, sneaky photos of you on the front pages of the tabloids, interviews, specialists asked for opinions, the lot! People will think you're a medium or clairvoyant – and if the Salcombe thing leaks out it will be a full-blown disaster.'

Callista groans. 'I know! It's all I've been able to think about since it happened. But thank goodness this is a Bank Holiday weekend, so we won't get the full blast of it until Tuesday. Would you like to pretend to be me next week and run a diversion, so I can get to school unmolested?'

Becks makes a derisive snort. 'Don't be ridiculous! I'm short and blond and slightly on the chubby side. You are least three inches taller, black haired and not remotely chubby – and please note that I remembered not to call you skinny. But we could make a plan – like we could leave for work really early and go in my car and not park in the teachers' parking area, we can park on the street behind the school and go in through the gate to the playing field.'

They have dinner and remain on the sofa for a couple of hours. Becks is insatiable when it comes to speculating about what happened in Callista's head, what she felt like, how scared she was when the gun went off and what might happen on Tuesday, and when they have finished the bottle of wine they go to bed after failing to come up with anything useful to keep Callista's life private.

. . .

'Good morning,' says Becks cheerfully the next morning. 'What a gorgeous day for a Bank Holiday Monday. Do you want to come for a run?' Then she looks carefully at Callista. 'Hey, what's happened? It's something bad, isn't it? I haven't checked if my phone has recovered yet, and I haven't used my laptop this morning – tell me what's wrong.'

Callista hands her own phone over, gets up and disappears into the bathroom. When she returns after a shower, Becks hands the phone back, visibly upset.

'Shit! It's erupted – it's incredible. Theories of different kinds are popping up everywhere, photos of you, opinions from scientists and rationalists and a Twitter feed where they suggest it is demonic possession and offer to exorcise the demon. I've never seen anything like it, not about a regular, normal person. Film stars and politicians would give a fortune for this kind of media exposure.'

'Not me – it terrifies me. Did you check my messages?'

'Of course, not – I would never do that. Or maybe I would - if I thought you had finally got over that ex-fiancé of yours and got yourself a new boyfriend. What are the messages like?'

Callista hands the phone back to Becks, says, 'Read them yourself,' and goes to make her breakfast.

'I don't much like the tone of this one.' Becks puts the phone beside Callista's plate ten minutes later. 'It

33

sounds nearly like a threat – or a warning of some kind. Well, we thought something about Salcombe might surface because of Okehampton. And the sender is just a phone number, not someone you've got saved as a contact - how the heck do these people get hold of your phone number?'

Thinking of Salcombe makes Callista feel slightly sick. 'God, I do hope they don't have a video of it! And remember, Rebecca Anne Simpson, that you promised never to mention it to anyone! Imagine the firestorm *that* would cause after this last event! I have no idea how they got my number – I don't like it at all. And it's not the only thing that worries me. Did you listen to the voice message from the producer of Up Close?'

Becks shakes her head and Callista plays the message on speaker, holding the phone out for Becks to listen.

'Hi, Callista, this is Gretchen Johnson. I'm the producer of the TV chat show Up Close that I'm sure you've heard about. We would love to have you as a guest on the show, Callista. I tried to call you a couple of times, but you must have had your phone turned off or been talking to people. So please call me back! Your extraordinary experience has fascinated the entire country and our viewers would love it if you would come in for a chat. Our next show is Monday week, ie one week from today, and we broadcast live. We are hoping to obtain more photos and video to make your story even more interesting. I look forward to hearing from you, bye!'

'Wow!' says Becks and takes the second piece of toast from Callista's plate. 'The little bit at the end about more photos and video, it sounds like they know they *can* get some more. She says 'obtain' – are they negotiating to buy someone's video? Because otherwise she would surely say that they're hoping to *find* more photos etc.'

'Becks, I keep telling you – just because we've known each other forever and we teach at the same school and your dad's uncle's brother-in-law, or whatever he was, was my mother's seventeenth cousin – it does *not* give you the right to steal my toast every second day. Go and make your own!' She snatches the half-eaten piece of toast out of Becks' hand. 'But I do agree – it sounds like she's trying a bit of mild coercion.'

She hopes that this little interlude will divert Becks from reverting to the message from the unknown sender, because that one makes her feel quite worried and she would rather not talk about it again just now. The message simply reads: 'And then there's Salcombe.'

35

Chapter 5

Before long Callista's phone is emitting a steady stream of alert beeps indicating messages, emails and calls. It starts just as Becks leaves for her weekend run, which not unusually has ended within twenty minutes at a café down by the water with someone she met on the way, and she sends a text message: 'Coffee with Debbie, don't answer door! Car with radio logo parked by number 47, white SUV, guy inside. Prob waiting for you to come out. Sorry, should have said earlier. Good thing my phone works again.'

She mutes the sound and puts the phone face down on the arm of the sofa, determined not to look at it for a couple of hours. While she makes a sandwich for lunch, she turns on the little radio in the kitchen and the two hosts of the chat show that Becks usually listens to are deep in a debate with a listener about the gun man at Okehampton.

'But listen!' says the caller. 'Whichever way you look at it and whatever that expert guy you have online might say, what's his name, Cosmo? This girl *must* be psychic – how the hell would she know he was going to pull out a gun otherwise? Nobody else saw it, it was inside his jacket, for Pete's sake.'

'I know,' says the female host, 'it's very puzzling. We've had a lot of feedback about this, lots of our listeners have been to our Facebook page and watched the video we posted, courtesy of Jack Milton, who sent it to us – it's the same as the one going viral everywhere. It's been viewed and shared eight hundred times in less than an hour since we first posted it and talked about it. And all the comments agree with you – this girl has some kind of gift, some ESP type thing. Let's hear from Cosmo now – he's been listening in and I'm sure he wants to have a say. What do you think, Cosmo? Apart from saying it can't have happened, which is the kind of the standard reply we expect from a sceptic or a rationalist.'

Callista stands as if nailed to the floor, her unfocused gaze on the loaf of bread in her hand as she waits to hear what Cosmo whatever-his-name-is will say.

A chuckle, a deep voice. 'Well, seeing you already

know what I'll say, we could perhaps discuss something else – what about the way the pound dropped in relation to the US dollar last week, I've been wondering about the reason for that.'

'You're always welcome to come in and discuss exchange rates, Cosmo,' says the male host smoothly, 'but seriously, what do you think about this incident at Okehampton? Do you believe it?'

'As you know I'm a rationalist, which basically means I believe in evidence and rational deduction. I have no explanation for this, but I would love to know more about it. I realise that most people consider that the video is evidence of thought transference of some kind, or perhaps people think that this girl's mind is like a receiver that happened to pick up something this guy's brain transmitted, just a one-off, as if they happened to be on the same wavelength for a moment – all sorts of things have been suggested already. I truly don't know what happened or how she herself experienced it, and as I said, I'd be very interested to talk to her. But for me to accept that it's some form of ESP, I'd require a lot more evidence and experimentation before I say it's possible. It's like when a scientist comes up with an astounding result from a single experiment – until it can be replicated, it might just be a fluke, an anomaly.'

The other host chips in, 'But how do you explain

what we saw in the video? And all the eyewitness statements support it – it did happen exactly as we see it in the video. There has been no editing, that's already been established by a specialist.'

'I don't know, and it's not for me to explain it. It looks like something most people would regard as evidence of ESP, but that doesn't mean anything to me. Something can look very convincing and turn out to be something completely different. There has never – not once that I'm aware of – been demonstrated that someone can literally read the thoughts in someone else's mind. The world if full of charlatans who set things up to convince an audience - and that's entertainment and to put it mildly, a money-making con job. Or people claim *after* an event that they had prophesized that it would happen, that's very common and sometimes I'm sure those people believe what they say. If she can replicate this, please invite me to a demonstration and I'll eat my words in public.'

Callista turns the radio off and thinks that Cosmo is an unusual name and she saw it somewhere not long ago in the context of fracking and earthquake clusters, so this might be another Cosmo. Forgetting the sandwich, she goes to check it on her phone, but when she lifts it and sees the message notifications, she feels overwhelmed and turns it off instead.

Why do I feel so conflicted about the stupid radio

show? she thinks and goes back to making her sandwich. From my point of view, I don't want the attention and the hype that is developing around this, I'd rather they all thought it was just chance, like some random piece of luck, that I had a crazy notion and the guy then turned out to really have a gun, perfect serendipity. But I also resent that Cosmo guy's attitude – fancy saying the video isn't proof! And that supercilious chuckle, that amused voice. He can't disprove it by being slightly sarcastic. Surely, he can see the sequence of events in the video, that culminates in me tackling that guy. What else could it be apart from some kind of damned ESP – not that I want to have it, and I really dislike it when all those idiots refer to it as a gift or an ability. It's a curse, that's what it is. I don't believe in that rubbish, I never did.

The call from the *Up Close* producer takes her by surprise because it comes on the landline phone they hardly ever use. So, when the phone on the kitchen bench rings, she lifts the receiver without thinking and listens to the exuberant greeting from the woman at the other end.

'It's Gretchen Johnson here, I sent you a couple of messages, or maybe three or four! Oh, I'm so glad I got hold of you, Callista! I'm sure you are *swamped* with calls and messages – you're a sensation, my dear, and a *heroine*. Ronald, you know our host of course, is dying for me to get you on the show, he's mesmerized by the video. I'm sure he spent an hour this morning just watching it over and over!'

She laughs, a high-pitched girlie laugh, which Callista instantly decides she detests more than any laugh she ever heard, and Gretchen continues without waiting for an answer. 'We'd *love* you to come on the show next week – we'll air the video again of course, and some more material might well come along, these days everything is being filmed by someone, doesn't matter where it is. And just hearing you talk about it would be so *interesting*. Ronald thinks we might get some great feedback – who knows what will come up, we might need to have you back more than once. You're *famous*, my dear!'

Callista's mind is working on two levels right through this over-the-top monologue. She listens as Gretchen raves on without needing any input from her, and at the same time she tries to weigh up the potential for harm. If they have heard of, or already have that vaguely referred to additional material, what is it? If it's something from the Salcombe incident she must be prepared with some low-key explanation, but if they don't have it, going on the show before someone sends it in – if it does indeed exist – might be her chance to damp down the madness, her chance to possibly defuse the Salcombe story, like a preemptive strike. Maybe the only opportunity before something happens that she can't control, her chance to comment in a public arena. She will be in a far better position if she gets to have her say first, rather than commenting later, after it is already out there. If she refuses to go on the show and they do have video from Salcombe, then it will turn into something she can't control and there will be no stopping it.

'I would be pleased to come on the show,' she says and interrupts Gretchen's tale of how much money she could make from print media by exclusive contracts for print and how this doesn't preclude her being on TV. 'Would you send me the details of where and what time, and also what kind of things Ronald wants me to discuss?'

When she has given Gretchen her email address and the effusive thanks are over, she sits down and eats her sandwich deep in thought. They will obviously invite someone to comment, so I'll ask if there is going to be someone else present and who it is. I wonder if they tell you things like that, probably they don't – they want to spring it on you to see what happens. So, I must prepare for a couple of scenarios. Becks and I watched that show once a couple of years ago and it was so toxic and simplistic that we never watched it again - a perfect example of 'appealing to the lowest common denominator' – tabloid TV. I can't remember if they have people calling in or questions from the audience – no, wait, I don't even remember if there was an audience. I need to have a variety of responses in my head ready to pop out – I'll talk it through with Becks when she comes in.

Chapter 6

As she often does when she is surprised, Becks shouts, 'You what!? Are you crazy? That show is unmitigated sleaze. And after that anonymous text? What if they have video from Salcombe? Perhaps they'll bring in someone who was there, who witnessed the whole event. Anything could happen – *please* don't do this!'

Callista is surprised by the level of Becks' concern; she knew Becks would probably be surprised by her plan, but not that she would be so vehemently against it. It makes her feel guilty, but she knows she is right.

'But I had to, Becks, I had no choice. Let's make a mug of tea and sit down and I'll explain it to you.'

They are still standing in the little hallway, where Callista has just opened the door for Becks who went running without her key; another thing that frequently happens. For some reason she blurted out the news about the call from the TV producer before Becks had even closed the door behind her.

I suspected she would be against it - I hope explaining it to her will make her understand my reasoning about how important it is to grab my chance to get in first. And anyway, talking about it with Becks might make me feel confident that I've made the right decision.

'This isn't the right place to discuss it,' she says, hoping her own doubts don't show. 'And I can see you haven't run very far, you're not even sweaty, so you don't need a shower right away. As my Mum says, everything is easier to explain over a glass of wine, but it's too early for wine, so I'll make us cup of tea.'

Behind her, as she turns to the kitchen, Becks says indignantly, 'What do you mean I haven't run far? I have so! I went right down and around the cathedral – a least a couple of miles, maybe three.'

'You've run a couple of miles? No way – you walked back up the hill, didn't you, slowly and talking to some bloke you picked up on the way?'

And Becks giggles and punches Callista hard in the upper arm. 'You're a witch, aren't you? A raven-haired, blue-eyed witch with psychic powers. A few hundred years ago they would have burnt you at the stake in the town square.'

'They might still do that if this takes off. But no – I

just happened to be looking out the kitchen window a minute ago and saw you come walking along at a leisurely pace, chatting to a guy I've never seen before - and he wasn't dressed for running, he looked more like he was on his way home from church.'

She turns the electric kettle on and gets mugs out from the cupboard, waiting to hear what Becks is going to say. The silence that follows her last statement is disconcerting; Becks nearly always forms rapid conclusions and never hesitates to state her opinion.

'You *are* psychic! That's exactly what he was – or is. He was just ahead of me when I came out of Cathedral Close and I went to run around him, and he heard my footsteps and took a step in the same direction, and I ran smack bang into him.'

'So, you didn't plan to meet him, you just bumped into him?' Callista turns to look at Becks. 'Pun intended. Can you get the milk out please?'

'He is a chorister at the cathedral, he'd just been to practice, and he lives quite near us, so we walked up the hill together.'

As soon as they sit down in the living room Callista returns to the subject of the TV show. 'Becks, listen! I do know that show is sleaze and innuendo, and we despise the creeps who put it together every week, and we've agreed it's the worst kind of tabloid style TV. But try looking at it like this – I must be prepared for something to emerge about the Salcombe incident, it's

46

nearly inevitable now when half the country knows my face - and remember that anonymous text message - it could happen any time, but I hope it won't until I've been on that damn show.'

She studies Becks' worried face over the edge of the mug and smiles. 'Even if it isn't a photo or a video - it might just be someone who calls the media and says, "I recognized her immediately, let me tell you what happened in Salcombe last year". So rather than let it take me by surprise, I thought dealing with it in my own way would be good, like a pre-emptive strike. I can prepare calm and undramatic things to say, try to defuse it before the first time it comes up – and this might be that opportunity! This live show next week is that opportunity – I'm sure of it. You should have heard the loaded things that producer said, full of implications. I think they know *something*, but she wasn't going to tell me - maybe they've been told about a video and are searching for it. It might be my only chance to make a statement rather than answer probing questions!'

'So, are you writing alternative scripts in your head, and constructing answers to whatever might come up? That might work.' Becks drinks some of her tea and studies Callista as if she doesn't quite believe her. 'But if there is video – that would be the worst. I remember how you described it to me, the way it hurt your head and that you stopped and put your hands to your temples. If someone has that on video, you're toast, darling. It's exactly what happened again at Okehampton. And if they have that, you can't deflect them with any calm and reasoned replies, they'll be all over you like a rash. No point in trying to say you were just walking past and nearly got hit.'

'Yeah, that would be the worst.' Callista knows a video might make all her reasoned statements and comments useless. 'In fact, that would make it impossible to defuse it at all. But how likely is it that someone got the whole thing from the very start on camera? It's far more likely that someone was alerted to start filming by the scream of tyres, and saw me grab that girl's arm, in which case I'll say, "Oh no, but I can't have. I'm sure I'd remember doing that." Or it could be that someone filmed the scene after it happened and saw me on the scene, either on the ground or standing there, and now they've recognized me. In which case I say, "Yes, it was very frightening to have it happen so close to me, and I'm so sorry for those poor people who were injured. I just got a cut on my arm." Don't you think that sounds like a good strategy?'

'Great plan,' says Becks and gets up to take her mug to the kitchen. 'But we all know that saying about the best laid plans, so I'll keep all my fingers and toes and other appendages crossed while I watch the show. And we'll have to hope nothing about Salcombe surfaces during the week. But now I've got to have that shower and change, or I'll be late for lunch.'

'The chorister?'

'Of course - he's very cute and very serious minded, and I want to get to know him better – he's nearly irresistible. Cute and serious will be good for me, instead of handsome and shallow, or handsome and bragging. I've been beginning to think lately that I must go for real quality instead of falling for pretty faces. I'll tell you later.'

'This isn't very early,' says Callista the next morning. 'I thought we'd try to get away a bit earlier than this – I hope there isn't anyone waiting out there.' She locks the door behind them and follows Becks down the stairs. 'We'll have to take your car - my battery's flat. I presume we're going to park in the street behind the sports field?'

'Of course – I even drove past last night on my way home to check they leave that gate unlocked overnight, and they do.'

'Where were you? You went out for lunch, didn't come home for dinner and then came in very late for a night before a working day, late even for you,' says Callista as they get into Beck's car.

'Could you try to sound a bit less like my mother? It was only a bit late, I got in just before one. Do you want the unvarnished truth, or would you prefer a euphemism?'

'The truth please – if you think I can handle it.'

'I was in bed with a choir boy.' They look at each other and laugh.

Chapter 7

In the days after the Bank Holiday, public interest turns into exactly the media frenzy Becks predicted. Psychologists are asked for their opinion, historians delve into the history of Okehampton Castle, and groups who dabble in the occult try to link the event to the site's ancient history. Radio chat shows air the topic every day and are commented on endlessly in the staff room at school. Becks makes it her mission to warn those on the staff, who can't leave the subject alone even when Callista is present and tells them in no uncertain terms that Callista needs no more attention, she already can't sleep properly at night, and to give her some space.

'It's not as if she wanted this to happen or made it happen,' she admonishes those she hears talking about it. 'You have to respect her wish not to be reminded of it all the time. She found it very scary, and she has no idea what it is or how it works. So please don't remind her of it every time you see her – she's not a freak show!'

On Wednesday morning the doorbell goes just after seven, and Becks opens the door in her PJs to find a serious-looking elderly couple asking for Callista.

'Who are you? And why do you want to talk to her? Do you realise it's very early in the morning and we have to get ready for work?'

Callista remains in the bathroom and listens through a crack in the door hoping Becks can get rid of them.

'I'm sorry to disturb you,' says the man, sincere and apologetic. 'We thought we might not be able to talk to her unless we tried really early – we have things to do too, but we're hoping she might be able to help us with something.'

'Well, you can't talk to her. She's in the bathroom and she doesn't have time. Let me give you my email address and you can send a question or two and I'll pass them on to her.'

'We just want to ask her if she could ...'

But Becks interrupts him firmly, but kindly. 'No, she can't. But I'll write down my email address for you and then I'm closing this door.'

Brilliant, thinks Callista, you're so smart Becks, you're just what I need at the moment. Imagine if I had opened the door – I'd be stuck there listening to them and worrying about being rude if I told them to bugger off.

A couple of minutes later Becks has given them the email address and the couple leave, with a final reminder from Becks not to come back and bother Callista in her home.

'Thank you!' says Callista over breakfast. 'That was brilliant – just about the only thing people haven't found out already is where my parents live and my own email address. Every other detail of my life is public property. I hope they won't pester you by email now.'

'I know how to get rid of them, if they continue sending me emails,' says Becks and grins. 'The first time I'll reply with whatever you tell me to say, or you can just type it in yourself, and if they come back with more questions, I'll consign them to the Spam folder where they can stay.'

That night while Becks is making her favourite dinner, pasta with smoked salmon and spinach in a cream sauce, and Callista is marking papers at the table, her mother calls.

'Hang on, Mum – I'll just close the door to the

kitchen, Becks has the fan on, and it makes a hideous noise.'

'We've had two phone calls and one reporter on the doorstep,' says Liz. 'Your dad opened the door and had a very amusing conversation with the man – thank God, he didn't invite him in – I thought for a moment that he would, they got on so well that it was turning into a friendship on the spot.'

She laughs, and as is mostly the case, she is amused by his eccentric interactions with the world. 'He engaged the chap in a deep and meaningful conversation about the development of young children into adults, and how the talents and trends you see in a child under twelve often don't develops into anything, and he quoted a number of stories of children with musical talents, like that superb student of his who became an aircraft engineer and never touched a cello after the age of fourteen.'

'And did the reporter leave after that, exhausted, side-tracked and confused? In that slightly baffled state that a lot of people experience after chatting to Dad.'

Callista smiles when she pictures her father embarking on a diversion, and Liz says, 'Oh, yes, the poor chap stumbled down the path, probably couldn't remember why he had come in the first place, but the funniest thing was that your father didn't do it on purpose. I thought he had, when I listened to it from the living room – but no, it was just one of those mad things that happen sometimes when he gets into a subject and won't let go.'

'And the phone calls, were they from the press or the lunatic fringe-dwellers?'

'One of each. You might hear from a man with a Welsh accent, who is the convener, as he calls it, of a group of Druid enthusiasts - he said he coordinates events at stone circles at various significant times of the year, like Stonehenge at the solstice. He thought this would be a good recommendation and make me trust him, and he was quite surprised when it didn't. He was perfectly nice when I said I couldn't give him your contact details and he said he would try to find out how to get in touch with you by other means. Probably casting runes and divining your phone number by the full moon or something of that kind.'

'You are the best, Mum - I feel totally relaxed and cheered up now. Bye!'

And she does; the fact that her parents seem to take it in their stride is a huge relief compared to how bad she would feel if they felt under siege or got stressed about her. She goes to tell the story to Becks in the kitchen and Becks laughs at the thought of Callista's dad side-tracking the reporter.

'I love your dad,' she says. 'Can you get the plates out please - this is ready now. He's like some character in a novel, maybe some eccentric Dickens personality. My dad is such a career animal — always after some deal or a merger or something, very little focus on the family. He wouldn't be able to handle this at all if it happened to me.'

Becks and Callista drive to school early the next morning, taking a different route and parking a couple of blocks further away. Just before they turn the last corner a news item on the radio catches Callista's attention, and she holds her hand up to stop Becks in mid-sentence.

'... but the police say that there is no case against Miss Bannister, who risked her life to save the children. These rumours are unfounded and spread by malicious bloggers. Anyone who wants to contact police with genuine information about the man involved in the incident at Okehampton Castle, particularly any information about where he got the gun, should contact Constable Yung at Exeter police on the following number ...'

'Good lord, what was that about? Please don't tell me they've got me down as an accomplice now!'

Becks shakes her head. 'I have no idea – I didn't catch the first bit. Let's have a look.' She parks, gets her phone out and gets busy searching for news, while Callista sits staring straight ahead.

'Nothing too bad,' she says after a few minutes. 'Do

you want to read it for yourself, or do you want the concise version?'

'Tell me, please! I want the shortest version possible.'

'OK, then, here it is. Someone from a group of people, clearly conspiracy nutters, who call themselves the Open Justice Coalition or the OJC, have posted comments on a couple of blogs saying that the reason the police won't meet with them to discuss the Okehampton case, is that they think you were involved with the gun man, but you panicked at the last moment. They claim the police don't believe what they call the simplistic version i.e. that the man they have under arrest, who is currently in a mental facility, was the sole person involved. The OJC demands the police make all files relating to this public for all to see.'

'Oh, God! this is going to drive me crazy – I'll have to change my name or emigrate, it will never end!'

'Of course, it will! Six months from now nobody will remember it – or only as a story from some vague previous year that they can't put their finger on – they'll say, "wasn't that two years ago, or maybe it was three". People are so flooded with info these days, that nothing really registers.'

They walk to the school sports ground gate without talking. Callista is visibly anxious, and Becks keeps glancing at her, worried. She knows there is nothing she can do to shield Callista from the speculations in the media and she feels increasingly helpless, unable to think of anything that will help.

'Callista, have you got a moment?' The Head comes up behind Callista and Becks in the corridor outside the staff room on Thursday morning, and it is obvious that he is unusually serious, and his request is only a question in form, it is actually an order.

'My office would be best, I think.'

Becks gives Callista an encouraging glance as they walk away and watches them until they disappear into the Head's office. She wonders what this is about, but she presumes that more stress is going to be added to Callista's already heavy load. She stands there for a couple minutes debating with herself if she should wait and decides that it would signal too much concern, and maybe make Callista feel responsible for Becks' stress as well as her own.

'Now then – I'm sure you know what this is about.' The Head looks across his desk and smiles in a way that has nothing to do with joy; it is a mixture of reluctance and embarrassment. 'I know this is a difficult time for you and you are being plagued by people wherever you go – and I do sympathize, I really do! You are being hounded by media and discussed as if you were a public person through doing something brave, saving lives. But the school is being increasingly affected too.'

'I know – I've had to use the sports field gate this week to avoid being caught. Is it a problem for the students? Are they being asked questions about me?'

'I haven't had any complaints about it directly from the students, but the parents are objecting to their children running the gauntlet of the press at the school gates – it seems to be particularly bad in the mornings. Some parents say that they feel the privacy of their children is being compromised. I'm not sure what we can do about it – have you got any suggestions?'

What a ridiculous question, thinks Callista and tries to look as if the is searching her mind for an answer. What could I suggest – apart from resigning or taking unpaid leave? I wonder if that's what he hopes I'll say. But I don't want to go on unpaid leave, why should I? It's not my fault this situation has arisen, I did something that was basically a good deed, so why should I be penalized for it?

Aloud she says, 'I can't think of any solution apart from simply riding it out. It's not as if I have done something bad, and I think any other action than just waiting for it to be over would imply that I'm being punished. This intense interest will probably die a natural death soon – don't you think? Something more exciting or novel will crop up and I'll be forgotten.'

Obviously, the Head was hoping that she would

take a different stance, but the way she phrased her reply has made it clear that she will not accept a suggestion from his side that she should take any form of leave. He nods and thanks her for her time, and when she turns in the door their eyes meet and she sees his unspoken acknowledgement; she has won, at least for now.

He will be aware of the staunch support I would get from the union, thinks Callista as she hurries towards the staff room, and it could backfire with really bad PR for St Michael's if the press decided to champion my cause. Imagine what wonderful headlines could appear; someone, who has done what I did being penalized by their employer. Stuff those parents! Having media at the entrance to the school won't traumatize their children.

A vague idea comes to Callista while she watches a physics class take a short test in the first period, and during the course of the morning she refines it and decides on her tactics. There are unseen forces and allegiances at St Michael's, and she knows who to involve in the execution of her idea for greatest effect. In the lunchbreak she walks down the hall to the administration office and asks to speak to Miss Watson, who has been at St Michael's longer than anyone, and who is famous for having told the Head to rewrite a form he wanted typed up and printed, on the basis that it was badly thought out.

'He got a "could do better" from Miss Watson,' said a teacher who had been privileged to be within earshot of the exchange, and though it is now three years ago, the story is often told to newcomers, when Miss Watson's name comes up in conversation.

'Miss Bannister, you asked for me?' Miss Watson is tall and thin and wears her grey hair in a not-quite pudding basin cut, which looks very good on her and has caused many comments on the lines of 'she hasn't changed her hairstyle since Mary Quant was the queen of fashion'.

Callista outlines what she thinks might be needed and manages to convey the subject of the conversation she had with the Head that morning without actually telling Miss Watson about it in detail.

'Aha, I see,' says Miss Watson, who is known for not wasting words, but Callista thinks she sees a little twitch at the corner of her mouth. 'Let me see what I can come up with. Have a look when you leave this afternoon. I'm sure we have all that we need in the supply room – we have materials for emergencies of various kinds.'

'Where did you disappear to?' asks Becks when Callista returns to the staff room. 'You haven't even eaten your lunch. Is something wrong? Is it to do with what he Head said this morning?'

'Kind of – I've enlisted Miss Watson. If she can't

fix it, nobody can. And who would dare tell her not to? Anyone here you can think of?'

Becks laughs, relieved to see Callista so upbeat. 'I think I can see where this is going! Very clever thinking – when can we see the result?'

'We'll go for a drive later and cruise past the main entrance after everyone has left for the day, so we can have a look.'

She refuses to tell Becks what she suggested to Miss Watson, only saying that she had a vague idea and left it for Miss Watson to develop further, and at the end of the day they leave the way they came, by the sports field gate.

Shortly before dinner they get into Becks' car and drive to the school, find a space to park and walk toward the main entrance. Yellow and black vinyl tape has been stuck to the pavement outlining a large rectangle whose sides join up with the stone wall, well away from the gates and extending to the edge of the pavement. Two large, laminated signs on bright yellow paper have been tied to the stone pillars flanking the entrance and printed on them in black letters is the text: 'Respect our students' privacy! This entrance is for students, staff and parents only. No media permitted inside the yellow outline. Trespass orders will follow infringements. Please note CCTV camera.'

'Do you know, I've never noticed that we had a CCTV camera at the gate before – that's very convenient. Not that I believe for a moment that the school could get trespass orders against people standing on the pavement,' says Becks and takes a photo of the security camera and the sign just below it. And what a great job they've done – all to Miss Watson's exact specifications, I'm sure. I bet her office had fun with this.'

'It's perfect!' says Callista. 'I wonder if the Head has seen it yet – probably not. He parks at the back and drives out that way – I don't think he ever uses the main gate.'

Becks takes two more photos and says she will post them on social media. 'I'll make a comment saying what a supportive school this is and how St Michael's isn't about to let staff and student be intimidated by reporters – and then someone will share it and the Head will be so pleased with himself!'

'I think I'll buy some flowers for Miss Watson. I'll order them online tonight.'

'Oh, don't! What if the Head thinks they're for the school and grabs them for his office?'

'OK, I'll bake a big batch of chocolate brownies for her. We've got that round biscuit tin, remember the one with a picture of Exeter castle that I got when I won the food basket in the Scout raffle? I'll put them in that.'

'Do you think she likes chocolate brownies? All she ever has for lunch seems to be a single sandwich – and some days she doesn't eat in the staff room at all. Bet she's never eaten a chocolate brownie in her life.'

'Don't be an idiot, Becks - everyone likes chocolate brownies.'

By morning break the next day photos of St Michaels' entrance have been shared several hundred times on Facebook and Instagram; it seems as if every student at the school took a photo when they arrived that morning. When Callista goes to the school office she finds Miss Watson in the stationery room stacking boxes of copy paper.

'Good morning!' she says and hands the tin over. 'This is just a little thank you present for that splendid effort. I hope you didn't get into trouble with the Head?'

'Thank you! Oh, no – no trouble at all – he's very pleased with himself this morning,' says Miss Watson blandly. 'Parents have already called to thank him for doing what he can to prevent the press from harassing the students.'

Callista returns to the staff room trying to decide if Miss Watson actually winked or if she just imagined it.

Chapter 8

Callista and Becks have just finished lunch and are quietly reading in their respective corners of the sofa, when Becks gets a message on her phone. 'Party time!' she says. 'Just what we need – a bit of fun without any hassles or reminders of strain and stress.'

She holds her phone out towards Callista. 'Remember Morgan, the Welsh guy I went out with a couple of years ago? He's having a housewarming party tonight and we're both invited – he says to bring whatever we want to drink and a salad, everything else is already organised by others.'

'Did he move, or has he bought a house? Are you taking the choir boy?'

'No, I'm not taking the choir boy – he's busy with his cricket team tonight, a boys-only event. He got married and they've just bought a house, Morgan, I mean, and I bumped into them a few weeks ago at Crockett's – they were coming in and I was leaving, we met in the door and didn't talk for long. They said they would have a party as soon as they had unpacked everything in the new house. I hadn't met his wife before, she shorter than I am, which made me rather like her.'

'Really? How come we're such good friends then?'

'Probably because we met when we were five years old, and in those days I was taller than you.'

The door to the narrow, terraced house in Saxon Road is wide open that evening when Becks and Callista arrive, and they can hear voices and music, so they walk in and find a kitchen-cum-living room crammed full of people.

'No point trying to introduce you to anyone,' says Morgan, who spots them coming through the door from the hallway. 'We've invited far too many people and we need a bigger house already. Come and meet my wife and then we'll let everyone take care of their own introductions.'

He takes the salad bowl from Callista, deposits it on the kitchen bench and calls loudly, 'Hey, Trish! Over here!'

A very short girl with the biggest brown eyes Callista has ever seen, like a Disney cartoon deer, materializes from the crowd and says, 'I'm sure the people six houses down the street heard you, Morgan. I was only a few feet away.'

'But I can never see you in a crowd, you just disappear.' He laughs and pats the top of her head. 'And if I yell, you always turn up. Callista, this is Trish.'

'I recognize you from somewhere,' says Trish and studies Callista intently. 'Now, where have I seen you – quite recently?'

I never know what to say when this happens, thinks Callista, I can't go anywhere now without somebody staring – I really don't want to talk about it right now.

Becks says casually, 'You probably saw her on YouTube or social media – but if you don't mind, talking about it is *not* what she needs right now. She's had more attention than she can cope with lately. And if you hear any others discussing her tonight, please shut it down – or call me, I know how to do it.'

And Trish graciously refrains from asking questions, orders Morgan to get some more glasses out and disappears behind them to check on something in the oven.

From then on, the evening develops into a slowly swirling mass of people, who group and regroup, see someone they want to talk to and turn sideways to slide between people. Becks gets absorbed into conversations, moves to another group, disappears from the living room into the hallway and reappears an hour later from the hallway into the kitchen end of the room. She sees Callista standing by the breakfast counter and laughs. 'Have you been here all the time since we arrived? Do you want me to introduce you to some new people I just met?'

And Callista smiles, amused at how their different techniques have achieved the same thing. 'Note where I'm standing, please – by the bar. I have probably talked to and got to know more people than you have, without moving more than a few inches this way or that. They all come here sooner or later.'

'Smart-arse!' says Becks, fills her wineglass and sets out on another round.

'That was amusing,' says a voice beside Callista. 'Excuse me for eavesdropping, but I couldn't help hearing it. I'm Patrick. And I could have predicted which one of you would be the strategic one staying put, and which one would be cruising the room.'

She studies his friendly blue-eyed face and smiles. 'I'm Callista,' she says and waits for a reaction, but there is no sign of anything being triggered in that handsome blond head. 'Are you a friend of the bride or the groom, so to speak?'

'The bride is my younger sister,' says Patrick. 'For my sins – I have spent years moving her gear from one flat to another and now finally into a house. And you?'

'Friend of the groom's former girlfriend, the one you just saw – pretty tenuous, but it got me invited.'

'He does pick short ones,' says Patrick and they both laugh. Twenty minutes later a buffet supper is set out and they continue the conversation sitting on the floor beside the couch with their plates and glasses, and Callista catches a wink from Becks and ignores it. When they leave, he asks for her phone number and Callista thinks that he is the nicest man she has met for a long while and hopes he will call her; a date with someone nice and funny would be the perfect diversion after a week of intermittent stress.

'Saturday – what bliss!' says Becks when she appears in her PJs at ten the next morning. 'That was fun last night – who was the blond guy? He seemed very taken with you.'

'Morgan's wife's brother – Patrick. What was her name again?'

'Trish – well, Patricia really, would you believe it? Their parents obviously never thought of how inconvenient it would be if they both ended up being called Pat. I saw him putting your number in his phone – are you going out with him?'

'I wouldn't mind. I talked to him for quite a while and he didn't recognize me, which is such a bonus – I might manage to spend an evening with him and not hear a word about Okehampton. Aren't you going for a run this morning?'

'No time for that! I'm having brunch with Dudley at The Old Firehouse; I must get a move on, or I'll be late. He's coming past at eleven – we're walking, he walks everywhere and when I said I'd pick him up, he said he'd rather walk, so that's what we're doing.' She thinks for a moment and adds, 'But when you think about it, he's quite right – he said he doesn't understand the logic of driving everywhere during the week and then going for a run in the weekend to keep fit.'

Callista looks thoughtfully after her when she disappears into the bathroom and wonders if this new romance with Dudley is serious – everything about it is very different from Becks' normal way of dealing with boyfriends where she usually makes the rules and picks up and discards men as she pleases.

A text message from Patrick comes just after Becks has left to meet Dudley and it takes Callista by surprise by its length.

It was great meeting you last night, just what I needed, ages since I met someone new and lovely. Would you like a casual meal tonight at the Prospect? It's a nice location down by the river, you've probably been there. I'll pick you up if you tell me your address. Patrick PS Tonight is on me

At half past seven she is sitting in The Prospect with a glass of chardonnay in front of her reading the menu and feeling so pleasantly anonymous that it is like being in an alternative universe. When Patrick picked her up there was nobody waiting outside the flat and nobody tried to waylay her as she came out, so there was no need to explain anything to this rare phenomenon, a person who has not heard of her. Being with someone who knows nothing about her so-called fame is a thing to treasure, and she wants nothing to ruin the evening.

'They do a really good lasagna here,' says Patrick, 'but I don't think I'll bother with the menu. I know this place well and they do the best fish and chips in town, so I'll go for that.'

He's such a happy looking chap, thinks Calista and smiles back at him. That a blue-eyed, blond look, like an overgrown schoolboy, is so appealing. Isn't it funny, I don't even know what he does, I must ask him.

'I don't know if you're a dessert eater,' says Patrick. 'I hardly dare ask – most girls these days seem to shy away from desserts. But if you haven't already tasted it, they do a layered walnut cake that's better than good. Only about a thousand calories per helping, so nothing to worry about. But we can order dessert later.'

The waiter takes the order and Patrick gets his phone out and says apologetically, 'I hope you don't mind, but I've just remembered I didn't tell my mother that I picked up the cushions Matalan ordered for her - and if I don't tell her that I've done it, she's bound to call me while we're eating. I'll just send her a brief text.'

'You were right – this is the best fish and chips I've had for ages,' says Callista half an hour later, after tasting the huge helping in front of her. 'I've been here before, but I hadn't tried them.'

'Last night after you had left, I asked Morgan why I had such a strong impression I had met you before – I thought maybe you worked in some business I go to, and he told me about your extraordinary experience at Okehampton. So, I have to confess that I spent some time looking it up on the internet – I wasn't spying, just fascinated.'

He smiles and she can't help smiling back, even though she feels disappointed that she is no longer anonymous in his eyes, but at least he didn't launch straight into the subject as soon as they sat down.

'It was a very odd experience, very confusing – but you've given me hope. I've been thinking that I would never meet anyone again who hadn't heard or read about it. The press won't leave me alone.'

'I can imagine!' Patrick raises his glass. 'Here's to the fifteen minutes of fame that someone said we all deserve – Andy Warhol, I think. The press will lay off after a while, but I must say it's fascinating – I never saw anything like it before, I mean the video from Okehampton. What did it feel like - if you don't mind talking about it? It looked painful.'

It is easy to talk to Patrick; he is genuinely interested and seems to understand how confusing the event was and how it has affected her, but suddenly he says, 'Sorry to interrupt you Callista, but a guy I play cricket with just spotted me, so I'll go and head him off – if I don't, he'll come over here and invite himself to join us and we'll never get rid of him - he's famous for it, and I can see he's a bit drunk already.'

This helping is for a giant, I've only eaten half of it and I'm full already, thinks Callista, and pushes her plate to one side and it nudges Patrick's phone that is still on the table. The screen lights up and she stares at the square red button that glows at the bottom of the screen and above it a line of text: 'recording – 48 min 23 sec'.

She has been taken in by a master of deceit. He pretended to be interested and claimed not to have heard about her experience until Morgan told him, she thinks, furious and disappointed. I bet that text message he said he had to send to his mother was a ruse, he just used the opportunity to start the recording, what a bastard!

She glances to the far side of the room; Patrick is talking to a man by the bar and not looking in her direction, so she slides the phone closer, stops the recording and deletes it.

What luck that his phone is the same as mine so I

know where to find everything, she thinks and picks the phone up, holds it low and scrolls up through the photos and finds two pictures of herself taken surreptitiously while he pretended to text his mother, so she deletes these too.

Another quick glance over towards Patrick, but he is still talking to his friend and now a couple have joined them and Patrick's back is towards her. And then it strikes her that the phone wasn't locked, the moment she touched it she was in, so she taps on the Setting icon, goes to Security settings, enters a screen lock PIN and turns the phone off.

On the way out she glances back at Patrick's phone, which is back in exactly the spot it was before she touched it, and smiles. She stands for a moment on the quayside by the Customs house and considers her first intention to go for a walk, but not the way they came, she wants to avoid Patrick. But she would rather get home as soon as possible, so she turns around and a few moments later she is on the path that runs through the greenbelt alongside the Roman wall. When she is out of sight from The Prospect, she stops, gets her phone out and calls Becks.

'Hi Becks - I hope I'm not interrupting anything romantic? Ok, good! Do you know Trish's maiden name? Or could you please ask Morgan for it?'

'What's going on? Is everything all right?'

'That bastard Patrick is either a journalist or a freelance reporter of some kind. He was recording our conversation and taking sneaky photos of me. I want to Google him to see which paper or radio station he works for.'

'Wow! How did you find out? And where are you now?'

Callista continues walking and tells the story about the plate nudging the phone and what she saw when the screen lit up.

'So, I deleted the recording and the photos and now I'm walking home.'

'You should have sunk his phone in his glass,' says Becks. 'What a bastard! I'll check on Facebook, I'm a FB friend of Morgan's and his wife will be on his page. I'll call you back.'

By the time Callista emerges at the far end of the greenbelt Becks calls back. 'Her surname is or was Carmichael, and I've Googled him – he's a freelance journalist, and he's provided articles and photos for The Sun in the past. Duds has met him! He's just beside me, I'll pass the phone over.'

'Hi Callista,' says Dudley. 'I think I've met this guy - is he blond and handsome, about thirty-five and plays cricket?'

'That's him – did Becks tell you what just happened?'

'She did. He's a total shit, by the sound of it. I met him at a veteran car rally last spring, he was with some people I know. What did you do when you found out – did you just walk out?'

'I'll let Becks tell you how I got to look at his phone, but I changed his code - you know, the PIN that unlocks the phone, and then I turned it off. And *then* I left.'

A shout of laughter from Dudley and Callista hears Becks in the background saying,

'What? What did she say? Tell me!'

Chapter 9

Becks and Dudley are sitting on the sofa drinking wine and watching 'The Time Traveller's Wife' on TV, which makes Callista laugh. Becks pauses the film and Dudley gets up, sturdy and ginger haired. This is the first time Callista meets him face to face and she is surprised at the size of him; he's much bigger than he seemed when she looked down from the kitchen window and saw Becks walking up the street beside him.

'Nice to meet you, Dudley. I see that Becks has started training you - she watches that film twice a year at least, she loves it.'

He laughs, 'I'm not suffering, I like it too and if I didn't, I could just read a book while she watches.'

'I think you need a drink after that drama. You

77

must tell us the whole thing - we're dying to hear it.' Becks disappears into the kitchen and returns with a wine bottle and a glass. 'When you called, I put this in the freezer to cool quickly – I thought you should have a glass of your favourite white, and our bottle is empty.' She pours the wine and subsides beside Dudley on the sofa. 'Right! What exactly happened? And don't leave anything out. And you can trust Duds, he is totally reliable.'

'Are you seriously going to call him Duds? I mean – Becks and Duds? It sounds like a comedy duo.'

Dudley glances at Becks and gives her a shove with his elbow. 'I know, just what I said – but it's what my mates call me, so it's pretty useless to try and get rid of the name now.'

'All right, you two!' says Becks. 'That's enough of that – tell us what happened please.'

'It was pretty undramatic,' says Callista and takes a sip of her wine. 'He picked me up and we went to The Prospect and had a glass of wine, and then he got his phone out and said that to avoid his mother calling in the middle of our meal to check if he had done an errand for her, he would text her. But of course, he didn't text her – not that I checked, but I'm sure it was just a way of getting an opportunity to turn the phone on to record. And while he had it in his hand, he took two photos of me too. And the story about the errand for his mother – it was so detailed and convincing, it sounded totally natural – some cushions he had picked up for her from Matalan, would you believe?'

She reaches for the bowl of salted almonds on the table. 'So, anyway, his phone screen was turned off, and the phone was on the table – kind of between us, just a bit to one side and there was nothing to show it was recording. While we were eating, he said that he'd asked Morgan why he felt he had seen me or met me before, and Morgan told him about Okehampton.'

'Devious bastard!' says Becks. 'He had it all planned in detail - every single move choreographed.'

'And he said nothing about Okehampton when he asked you out or when he picked you up?' asks Dudley. 'Did you think he didn't know about it, right up to that point?'

'I thought I had come across the only person in England who hadn't heard of me,' says Callista bitterly. 'I had no idea he's a freelance writer, I hadn't asked him what he does for a job – and he probably would have lied or been evasive anyway. I was hoping we would have a nice meal and talk about normal things – it would have been such a relief. And then he spotted some guy he knows coming in, and he said "I've got to head him off or he'll be wanting to sit down and talk to us and never leave" - and idiot that I am, I thought it was sweet that he didn't want our date to be interrupted. But of course, it was just that he didn't want our talk about Okehampton to be interrupted.'

'What sort of things did he ask? Were they media-type questions?' Becks is looking for options for damage control. 'I mean, did he get something new out of you that he'll be able to sell? Was he kind of leading you on to say things you might not have said if you'd known who he was?'

'God, yes! He was going for the sympathetic and understanding personal angle, wanting to know if it had affected my sleep, did I feel worried there was some strange thing going on in my brain, did my family believe me – all that sort of stuff that I would *never* have told him anything about, if I'd known who he really was.'

'And then you disabled his phone?' Dudley grins. 'I can't imagine how you thought of that just then – you must have been so angry.'

Becks smiles at Callista and says, 'She is super smart, Duds, she always was - right from when she was a little girl. You'll soon realise that she is the perfect person to be in a bad situation with - hardly ever loses her cool.'

'It was just a flash of inspiration – I stopped the recording, of course, and deleted it, and then I saw the photos, so I deleted those too. And in the last minute – I was just about to put the phone down and get up and leave – I thought how fitting it would be to punish him by putting a PIN on his phone, which surprisingly he didn't have already. And his phone is exactly like mine, so I didn't have to search – it took no more than ten seconds.'

'I'd love to have seen his face when he discovered,' says Becks gleefully. 'I can imagine him standing there wondering where you have gone and then after a while, he'll pick up the phone and realise what you have done. Brilliant! I'm so proud of you!'

'By the way, what did you use for a PIN?' asks Dudley. 'I find it really hard to come up with a new password or a PIN at short notice, my mind goes blank.'

'I used the atomic mass of silicon, which is 28.085, but I left out the decimal point of course.'

'Why silicon? Why not copper?'

'I don't know, I had to do it really quickly, in case he turned around or started back towards our table – in case I had to make a dash for it, if he saw me with his phone in my hand. Not that I actually thought about all that at the time, it was just a quick thought, seeing he didn't have a PIN, set one up that I couldn't forget. In case he turns up and threatens to sue me for malicious damage unless I unlock it for him – imagine not being able to remember exactly what it was! And I was talking to one of my classes only yesterday about silicon, so it just popped into my head - it's such an easy one to remember.'

. . .

'Callista – are you awake?' asks Becks the next morning and opens the bedroom door a crack. 'Could you come out here please.'

'If I wasn't already, I would be now. OK, I'm coming.'

It is half past eight, the sun is shining, and Dudley is sitting in the armchair by the window dressed in tartan boxer shorts and eating toast with Marmite; backlit by the early sun he looks as if he is covered in orange fur like a lion.

'Here she is now,' says Becks to someone on her phone and holds it out to Callista.

'Who is it?' she whispers, and Becks mouths, 'Morgan!'

Callista takes the phone, turns it to speaker mode and holds it in front of her, so Becks and Dudley can hear the conversation. 'Hi Morgan! Did you want to talk to me?'

'Yes, I have to – I'm very reluctantly advocating on behalf of my brother-in-law. And before you say anything, I would like to say that I'm embarrassed to have him in the family, so to speak. Trish and I are really upset about this –we had no idea that he did that sort of thing to get material for his articles. And to do it to someone he met at our house – that makes it even worse.'

'OK - and?'

'He needs to get into that phone, Callista, it's got all his contacts and emails, he can't afford a new phone and his laptop is on the blink – and he's too gutless to ask you what the PIN is.'

'Did he tell you what he did? Is he with you now?'

'Yes, he is here right now. And I think he told us everything because I said I wouldn't be the middleman unless he told us the whole story. He said he took sneak photos of you, tricked you into talking very personally about the Okehampton incident, recorded the conversation and so on – led you on to reveal more than you might have otherwise.'

'That sounds pretty accurate,' says Callista. 'But listen, turn your speaker on please, I want him to hear this first-hand. Is it on? OK then - I want one thing from him first. I'll give you my email address and I want Patrick to email me an apology, and in it I want him to list exactly what he did, every single step of the way. If he does that, I will email him the passcode. Can he log on to his own email on your computer? I want the email to come from his own account.'

'Yeah, sure. He can use my laptop and send it from his own account. And he says OK, he'll do what you ask – and he also says he'll delete everything relating to you, and he won't use it.'

'I deleted everything I could find last night. Tell him that if he mentions *anything* about what he and I talked about, even one single word, I will post his photo and his email

on social media with all the hashtags I can think of, and I'll ask everyone I know to share the post, OK? I can think of a lot of good hashtags to use, my imagination is working on it as we speak.'

She gives Morgan her email address and ends the call.

'Bravo!' says Dudley. 'You take no prisoners – well done. And it's nice to know the bastard heard what you said, straight from you.' He studies her for a moment and then he adds, 'You are very, very good at thinking on your feet. I'll be proud to become your nearly-but-not-quite-related brother-in-law.'

Callista stares, at first confused and then with an incredulous expression on her face as his meaning dawns on her. 'You didn't! Did you really – get engaged, I mean? You've only known each other for a couple of weeks.'

Becks snorts, 'You're not the only one who can think on your feet. I knew he was a treasure from the moment I bumped into him, and I'm not letting him get away.' She holds her ring finger up and wiggles her hand. 'Not a real engagement ring, but he made it himself.'

Callista takes her hand and looks closer. 'Is that the wire cage thing that holds the cork in a champagne bottle?' she says suspiciously. 'Did you have champagne last night? And there was none left for me?'

'Yep, that's what it is – I think it's a great ring. Who needs diamonds? And the wire cage as you call it, is actually called a muselet – bet you didn't know that! I'm sorry there wasn't any left for you, but we needed it for our celebration.'

Chapter 10

Callista is getting a jacket out of her wardrobe when she hears Becks exclaim, 'Oh no, we've run out of milk – bugger! Too many cups of coffee and Dudley likes lots of milk. I wish I'd noticed before he left for the cathedral – I could have asked him to drop some in on his way back. I just fancied a cup of tea before I go and have my shower.'

'I'll get some on my way home, I'll be back before lunchtime. Have some of that herbal tea you got – it doesn't need milk, does it?'

'I'm not drinking that stuff again - it smells of hay and tastes like compost, horrid! And where are you going at this time on a Sunday morning?'

Callista knows she must either tell Becks now and be subjected to a scene or lie about it and then feel awful when it comes out, as it is nearly sure to do. 'I'm having coffee with Harry.'

With an expression of barely contained fury Becks shouts. 'Are you crazy?! I can't believe it! Why are you having coffee with that bastard? Please don't tell me you're getting together with him again!'

'Of course, I'm not, nothing could be further from my mind – but he said he's got something to tell me and he wanted to do it face to face. He sent a text this morning, said he felt concerned about all the media hype about me and has some information he thought I should have.'

'Oh, please don't! He's just trying to get back together – remember how hard it was to get him to realise you didn't love him any longer. It was an affront to his vanity – he was supposed to be the one breaking up, not you! And he'd love to have you back. I always suspected he loved being seen with you – I don't mean he didn't love you in his own shallow way - but he took it as a personal compliment how people look at you because you're so beautiful. Oh, please don't go!'

Callista listens to this tirade, which is typical of Becks, and concentrates on trying to look calm and not show that she is quite nervous about meeting Harry again. Who knows if the spell he cast over her is still active or if it has been truly extinguished.

'It's just half an hour over a cup of coffee, Becks!

Please don't be so melodramatic – I'm not getting together with him again, no way! But I'm very curious about what he's heard. When I replied and said he could tell me by text, he said, "not the kind of thing I would like to tell anyone by text, too disturbing" and I agreed to meet him.'

Becks is staring at her, struggling with her intense dislike of Harry and her instinct to make sure Callista doesn't fall for his evil charm again. 'I'll come with you. I want to hear what he's going to tell you – and I can keep an eye on him. He knows I saw right through him from the start, he won't try anything if I'm there.'

'No way! I'm not a teenager, Becks! I can deal with him, and I don't need any help, but thank you for the offer. I promise, I'm totally over him.'

She smiles, but inside she wonders if any of the old infatuation will revive when she sits across from Harry again. The man who deceived her and cheated on her and once hit her very hard in a fit of fury, who cried and said he was sorry and promised never to do anything to hurt her again. I was such a fool, she thinks, but there was something about him that made me believe everything he said, or nearly everything. And I fell for it again and again, the remorse and the promises and the way he begged me to not leave him. I hope I'm immune now, but I've only seen him in the distance once or twice in the last year and I felt no attraction then, didn't regret breaking off with him, but at close quarters it might take a bit of resolution to resist that evil charm, as Becks calls it.

She deliberately picks a jacket she knows he dislikes, a denim biker-style jacket she has had since university and smiles at herself in the mirror. It will be like telling him I no longer dress to please him, that I no longer need to dress up to look smart and elegant, to impress his friends and his boss and make others envy him. My God, I can still remember the look on his face when he told me what his boss had said about me after we went out for drinks that time, how he took favourable comments about me as proof of his own taste, like a personal accolade.

She leaves with a brief 'bye' called out to Becks, who is in the bathroom, pleased to get away without any further drama and runs down the stairs, keen to get to the café before Harry does, to be the one to see him come in, to observe him before he sees her.

On the ground floor, just inside the door to the street, is a little brown paper parcel with a large white label tied on with string. It has been left so the label sits neatly on top with the text side out and on it is written in large capital letters, 'CALLISTA BANNISTER'.

She contemplates leaving it tucked away in the corner for when she comes back, but curiosity wins, she picks it up and takes it with her. Halfway down the hill she stops and studies the parcel in her hand; it has been wrapped in what is obviously used brown paper and the string around it is tied in a neat bow with the label attached through a hole punched in the stiff white card. Waiting until she is in the café or until she gets home is suddenly impossible, she must know what is in it, she cannot wait another moment.

She pulls the label off and stuffs it in her bag and slides the string off, folds the paper back and stops with a smothered exclamation of dismay. A cloth doll lies on the sheet of brown paper, and it is clearly meant to be her. A doll roughly the length of her hand, with long dark hair made of wool, tied at the back in a ponytail, with blue eyes drawn on the white face with marker pen and a long pin pushed through its head, from one temple to the other.

Callista stands as if frozen and stares at the doll with a mixture of revulsion and fear. Someone has gone to a lot of trouble to make a voodoo image of her and with malice and hatred pushed a pin though her head. She quickly wraps it in the paper again, reluctant to even touch it with her hands, winds the string around it and ties a tight knot to stop it unfolding. Should she throw it in a rubbish bin or keep it, show it to Becks, ask what she thinks she should do with it? Or should she drop it in at the police station and ask them to show it to Mary Yung? She can't make up her mind, so she pushes it into her shoulder bag and continues down to the town centre.

· · ·

Ten minutes later, still unsettled, she orders coffee and sits at a table by the window where she can see the door and waits for Harry to arrive. The parcel with the doll is still in her bag and she puts it on the floor, over to one side, as if distance will make it feel less menacing than having it close beside her. She spots Harry as he crosses the street on an angle, his wavy brown hair ruffled by the wind, as handsome as ever. He's wearing a tight grey t-shirt under a black jacket, and she thinks how strange it is, that clothes that on someone else would look ordinary, on him look smart and sexy.

The way his expression changes when he sees her already seated with a cup of coffee in front of her, makes her wonder if he is taking her early arrival as a sign of keenness on her part, as if the desire to see him has made her rush to get here. There is a certain satisfaction on his face, and she recognizes it — he is congratulating himself on something he sees as a victory.

He orders coffee and comes across the room and leans over to kiss her cheek, and she is intensely relieved that she feels no different than she would if any casual friend greeted her.

'Hi Harry,' she says politely, and gives him a little smile. 'How are you?'

His eyes sweep over her face, take in every detail and suddenly that well remembered habit of his makes her want to laugh. Never again will he ask why she hasn't done something different with her hair, why she is wearing that jacket and suggesting what she should have put on. And never again will she feel she has let him down, disappointed him and not done her best. The relief is intense and wipes all thoughts of the voodoo doll from her mind.

Harry sits down and says without preamble, 'I'm not enjoying bringing bad news, Callista, but I wasn't sure what was best – I could have gone to the police, but I thought you should decide for yourself what to do about it.'

He gets a folded sheet of paper out of his inside jacket pocket and hands it to her. 'This is a screenshot of a Twitter post – a friend directed me to it, knew it must be about you and thought I'd want to know.'

Unsure of what to expect and acutely aware that he is watching her read something that is obviously disturbing, makes her pull herself together, determined not to show any strong reaction and give him occasion to revel in whatever feeling it might engender in his vain heart.

She reads it silently to herself and then out loud, in a quiet voice. 'We know who she is, where she is, we have seen the video. She is dangerous and deceitful and must be stopped from fooling the public. She has no real magic. We know what's real, this isn't. If you see her, deal with her, prevent further damage.'

Harry's expression is serious, and she doesn't

understand why. 'Why does this worry you?' she asks. 'It's an odd tweet, but it's not threatening physical violence – it's just a bit off, isn't it?'

'That identity – fullmoonmagic – I checked it out. It's a woman called Vanessa Saunders and if you google her name, you'll find that she belongs to a group, at least one, of people who believe in black magic and spells and all kinds of nonsense. There is some quite disturbing stuff on the blog page her group runs.'

For a brief moment, just for a second, Callista nearly tells him about the doll in her bag, but common sense prevails. The last thing she needs is for Harry to dine out on this additional morsel of information, perhaps make out he is in her confidence, so she just looks thoughtfully at him and says, 'Thanks, Harry – I'll definitely take it to the police and let them deal with it.'

'I miss you,' he says abruptly, his eyes on hers. 'I really do, I miss you dreadfully. I wish you'd come back to me – would you please think about it? You would have my word that I would do better this time. I know I can – all those things, they were based on jealousy and insecurity.'

She regards him with a feeling of disbelief and knows he is the most accomplished habitual liar, or maybe self-deceiver, she has ever had the bad fortune to come across. He is far worse than Patrick; a species of human she can identify within five minutes of meeting these days, because two years with Harry made her an expert. The sort of person who never accepts responsibility for anything they do, but puts the blame on you, who shamelessly blames their own serial infidelities and violent outbursts of fury on jealousy or insecurity. No, he is not a simple conman like Patrick, but a complex, self-deceiving manipulator.

'No thanks, Harry. I'm over it now, but I hope you will find someone to be happy with. And thanks again for the warning.'

She gets up, lifts her bag from the floor and walks out the door without looking back, leaving him with his coffee untasted. Her feeling of liberation and calm is euphoric; she knows now that he has no power over her any longer, there is no remnant of attraction in her mind, it is truly over.

Returning to the flat with the milk and a large bar of dark chocolate with almonds, Callista debates with herself if she should show Becks the doll or simply give it to the police. But I need someone else to see it, she thinks, and if I'm going to hand it over today I need to go home and have lunch first anyway – I'm not turning around now and walking all the way back down to town.

Chapter 11

Becks has heard the downstairs door and footsteps coming up the stairs and is standing in the hall waiting for Callista. 'How did it go? Are you OK - or did you fall under the spell of His Sexy Majesty again?'

Callista smiles and hands her the milk. 'The spell doesn't exist any longer – totally gone, not a trace of it. I just looked at that handsome face and felt nothing. Or possibly I felt a bit of regret that I wasted two years on him, but on the other hand I learnt a lot.' She smiles as she follows Becks to the kitchen. 'Like how to spot a man of his type and how to break up with someone who protests undying love with tears on his cheeks. And how to *not* do everything to please someone else, who just wants to dominate me and abuse me. Is that enough to reassure you?'

They sit in their usual corners of the sofa with

coffee and a dish of the broken-up chocolate bar and Callista lifts her bag that she dropped on the floor when she first came in.

'First this,' she says and hands Becks the sheet with the screenshot of the tweet. 'Harry told me who this "fullmoonmagic" person is, so we'll get to that in a moment. He didn't say if he worked out where she's located, but I'm sure the police can find out. Because there's something worse that I must show you - and the two things might be connected.'

Callista sees Becks' eyes move to the brown paper parcel that sticks up from her bag. 'Yep, you're right, that's it – but since I first opened it, I've had second thoughts, so we'll be careful how we touch it.'

She reaches for the box on the table and pulls out a couple of tissues. 'I'll use these to handle it.' She wraps one tissue around her thumb and one around her fingers. 'Seeing we don't have vinyl gloves – I'm going to give this to the cops, but you must see it first.'

She lifts the parcel out and moves it awkwardly around until she can unfold the paper on the sofa cushion between them, and Becks draws in a breath of shocked surprise. 'My God!'

The little doll lies on her back with her painted blue eyes staring at the ceiling and the thick needle pushed through her head.

'I didn't notice that at first.' Callista marvels at her own calm voice. 'I thought it was a pin, but it's actually one of those darning needles with a big eye. What do you think?'

'That's pure evil! I never thought I would see one of those in real life – you read about them in books, but who makes them these days, and in this country? It's such a horrible and primitive way of frightening someone.'

'Not just frighten, though – it's supposed to actually do the same damage to you, that they inflicted on the doll, to hurt you physically by remote, so to speak - not just to scare you. I remember it from a film years ago; you saw the person holding the doll and sticking pins in it and you saw the person the doll represented writhing in agony, clutching the body part the needle went into.'

'Either somebody wants to hurt you or perhaps the needle represents that pain you feel - I mean, it could be that they've seen you in the video clutching your head, and it's obvious you're feeling pain. We must give it to the police – today!'

After lunch Becks drives them to the police station with the doll, the wrapping paper and the label in a large plastic zip-lock bag on the back seat and the printout of the tweet in Callista's bag. An hour and a half later they return to the car, feeling slightly overwhelmed and drive back to the flat where Callista opens a new packet of biscuits and makes coffee while Becks goes to the bathroom.

'If it wasn't half past three in the afternoon, I would open a bottle of wine – I had *no* idea they would be so damn thorough,' she says and raises her mug in a toast. 'I'm very impressed with the Constabulary – here's to them! And I'm also glad we took those photos of the doll and the label and the note Harry gave me – it would be quite easy to wake tomorrow morning and imagine it was all a dream.'

'Not a dream, a nightmare,' says Becks. 'I thought about it while they were doing all the stuff with the fingerprints – not that I ever touched that wrapping paper, but I suppose they did it just in case, to eliminate my prints too. I thought of how good it would be if the tweet and the doll are connected – because once they find that woman it takes care of two nasty things in one hit.'

'What an exciting weekend we've had,' says Becks that evening after supper when they sit in the living room drinking cocoa, which is a habit from their shared student days. 'A conman taking you out for dinner, then the most spectacular revenge ever devised by anyone – you did that *so* well. And me getting engaged with the help of the muselet from a bottle of champagne - could it get any more exciting and glamorous than that? And to top it off, the drama of the voodoo doll – and you meeting with Harry and not falling for him again.'

'Total drama right through, but here's the final instalment – read this,' says Callista and hands her phone to Becks, with her emails open. 'I got his apology while you made the cocoa - that scumbag really did himself proud!'

Becks reads Patrick's message and laughs, delighted with how well Callista's strategy worked. 'My God – that's what I would call abasing yourself, he's downright grovelling! Not that I believe that he will never do it again to anyone – of course he will, but that's a great list of sins and he even includes that bit about faking a text to his mother. You'll be able to hold this confession over his head forever.'

Callista laughs. 'But you haven't heard the best bit. I replied with the code to unlock his phone, and do you know what he did? Unbelievable - he replied with a "thank you!" followed by a heart symbol – he is a man *totally* lacking in judgment.'

She drinks some of her cocoa and sighs. 'Isn't this the best comfort drink on a rainy evening you could ever imagine? We've been doing this for so long – apart from that year I lived with Harry.'

'And now for the important part,' says Becks, when they have finished their cocoa, businesslike when it comes all matters of appearance. 'What are you going to wear tomorrow on that TV show? We must discuss it now because I honestly don't trust you to make the right choice.'

'Oh, for heaven's sake – I'll just wear jeans and a nice shirt or something. I think looking plain and ordinary is a good look – being unremarkable is such a good disguise to hide behind.'

'No, no, no! You're I *not* going to hide, that's the whole point and anyway, you'd find it hard to look unremarkable unless you wore a paper bag over your head. No, the whole point here is that you want to show the world that you are smart, educated and classy. Because what that sleazebag, what's his name? the host, anyway - what he probably wants to portray you as is someone either from the lunatic fringe or a revival hippie - or maybe someone a bit mental. You've got to convey that you dislike the attention, stress that you don't believe in all this extra-sensory stuff and not let him drag you down to his level. It's not just what you say and how you react, it's also how you look.'

Caught between her wish to play down her appearance and her long experience of how clever Becks is when it comes to clothes, Callista stops to consider. She might be right, she thinks, maybe people will have some preconceived idea of what I'm like – maybe they expect me to be a bit flaky, claiming to be a mystic of some kind or someone just after attention. And then I put them on the back foot by presenting a completely different image, something that doesn't fit with their expectations.

'Yes! You *are* right – I should look and sound smart, rational and career-minded. Let's go and have a look.'

They leave their mugs on the sofa table and head for Callista's bedroom.

'Sit on the bed,' orders Becks and opens the wardrobe door. 'Oh, my goodness – you are so tidy, it's nearly pathological. I'll never show you mine.'

She starts at the right side and pushes the hangers aside one by one, studies each item of clothing. 'This is possible.'

A lime green linen shirt lands on the bed beside Callista. 'And this one.' A black and white striped shirt follows the green one. 'Hey, I like this white shirt with the button-down collar. You haven't worn that for ages, and it really suits you - I remember when we bought it in that lovely shop in Bristol. Didn't you buy two? I think I remember a blue one the same.'

'That was the one that got ruined in Salcombe last year – the sleeve was cut, and the bloodstain never came out, it had dried by the time I got home.'

Near the end of the rail, she finds what she's looking for.

'This is it! Definitely – I know what we want now, I can see it in my mind. We'll go for super-sophisticated top half with causal, trendy bottom half and then we'll find the perfect shoes. This very elegant short jacket with the military braiding – God, it's just lovely and that's just what we need, it shouts classiness. So, you'll be kind of telling two stories at once - I'll show you. Start undressing and I'll pass you things.'

Callista pulls her jumper over her head and emerges laughing. 'We haven't done this since we were students, have we? Remember how we used to go through our combined supplies of clothes and pick out the best from both, when one of us was dating. I feel like I'm nineteen again.'

'You look like you're nineteen,' says Becks and hands her the white shirt with narrow black stripes. 'And your skinny black jeans, not the pre-faded ones - and now put the jacket on.'

'Boots or shoes?' asks Callista and studies what she can see of herself in the mirror. 'We'll have to go and look in your long mirror – I can't see the whole effect.'

'Those ankle boots, the biker-looking ones – you know the ones I mean, the black ones with the chains around the ankle and the very thick soles– where are they? I've hardly seen you wear them since you bought them.'

'In the shoebox in the corner, with the sneakers sitting on top.'

They go to Becks' room and study the result in the full-length mirror and Becks grins. 'Perfect! And those boots will be in the picture whenever the camera isn't on your face and they'll do that *je ne sais pas quoi* thing, like a statement saying, I'm classy and smart and beautiful, and I'll wear what I damn well please on my feet - I'm not a fashion slave. Don't you think?'

'Oh, yes - you are so clever Becks! And these clothes are comfortable – apart from this very formal jacket – but I can sit any way I like and not worry about my legs or my skirt. Do you think I should put my hair up in a classy bun or just pull it back in a ponytail?'

'Just wear it down or in a ponytail. Mixed messages, that's what we want, not some carefully composed whole where all the parts came out of the same box, but still very stylish.'

Chapter 12

Becks drops Callista at the flat after school on Monday and carries on to pick up Dudley early from his job in the bookshop. They are driving to Taunton for dinner with his parents and to stay the night.

'It makes it so real,' said Becks worriedly that morning when she packed an overnight bag. 'Going to meet his parents! I haven't got used to be being engaged yet and they must have been so surprised when he said he's engaged to someone they never heard him mention even! I hope I can behave properly right through a meal and not say something that ruins the impression he might have given them!'

Callista laughed at this uncharacteristic display of insecurity and said, 'Rebecca Anne Simpson, how could they possibly not love you from the moment they meet you?'

The drive to Plymouth takes less than an hour on a good day, but she plans to leave early and find the studio, park the car and then have a snack meal somewhere nearby.

'Please be here by half past seven,' said the producer in an email. 'That way we know we have plenty of time for a briefing and make-up and to make you familiar with the set. We like to give ourselves a bit of extra time for unforeseen events, like last minute toilet visits etc – particularly with the guest who's on first.'

Callista changes her clothes and decides not to have anything to eat, she would rather get to Plymouth and find a snack meal somewhere when she has parked the car and is within walking distance to the studio. At half past five she locks the flat and walks around the corner to where her car is parked, in the only street close by that always seems to have lots of space. But the car doesn't start; she turns the key several times and gets an increasingly weak response from the starter motor. Perhaps driving around for half an hour wasn't enough to charge the battery, she thinks, and now I've run it flat again, but the motor did turn over the first couple of times, maybe it's something else. And I don't have enough time to try to borrow a car from someone else. I should have taken it for a drive this morning before school and I would have discovered this.

She Googles the bus timetable and calls a taxi – the last thing she needs now is to make a hurried rush down to town and get hot and flustered. 'I want to go to the bus station,' she says to the driver. 'I'm in a hurry - I have to catch the bus to Plymouth and I have very little time.'

They make it with a few minutes to spare and with a sigh of relief she gets her ticket and boards the bus. It's nice going by bus, she consoles herself, as they drive out of Exeter. I haven't done it for ages, but you get to see things from a different perspective. I should be just in time to catch the last bus home, seeing I'm first up on the show – and no need to hang around in the studio after I've had my turn. I'll just leave straight away.

Taking a taxi from the bus station to the TV studio is the simplest way to get there, it is too far to walk, but there isn't enough time for a quick meal, so she stands in the doorway to an antique shop a few doors down the street and admires the elegant Regency desk in the window while she eats the chocolate bar she bought at the bus station.

· · ·

'I'm Ronald,' says the host of *Up Close* when Callista arrives and smiles his practiced camera smile, eyes crinkling and designer-stubbled cheeks creasing just the right amount to look like genuine enjoyment.

'How lovely to meet you in real life! Gretchen is unwell, so we have to manage without her – I know she'll be devastated to miss meeting you. But I'm thrilled to have you here! Such a great story and so much interest. You're just in time to be next in make-up, let me show you the way.'

He has an unmistakable aura of self-importance, and she gets the feeling that he thinks he doesn't really need to introduce himself because everyone knows who he is anyway; he only does it to demonstrate how modest he is.

I am prejudiced, thinks Callista, and I admit I was prepared to dislike him, but I had wondered if he would be different off screen than his on-screen persona, perhaps more genuine and nicer, but no – he is a nasty man.

Something about his greeting sends a little shiver down her spine; there is a quality of speculation in the way he looks her over. His eyes seem to measure her for fit, as if he has already constructed a custom-made pigeonhole for her, predetermined what she is like and how she will react. Don't be paranoid, she tells herself, you're just apprehensive and maybe he hadn't expected you to look like you do today, very different from the girl in the video from Okehampton, older, more self-assured perhaps and more stylish.

He shows her to a small room where one wall has a long mirror with very bright lights mounted above. It looks unnatural and glaring, but it might be to demonstrate what the studio lights will do to you, she thinks, and studies her pale image. If this is what you look like under the studio lights, then I understand why everyone needs to be made up by a professional, I look pale and featureless.

'Sit yourself down and let Carol do her thing - not that you need it, you look just gorgeous. I'll see you in ten for a bit of a briefing before we start.' He points at the empty chair on the right.

The man in the other chair studies her in the mirror and they exchange a smile before she sits down beside him. She doesn't know who he is, but he's got a nice smile.

And some additional attributes, she thinks, and tries not to look directly at him. Good looking and with some kind of something radiating out from him like a minor force field. Not just sexiness, something more, strength? I don't know what it is, but it is quite compelling. He must be one of the other guests for the piece after my interview, they said I'd be on first, and they have two other guests after me.

The girl removes the towel from the man's shoulders, and he gets up and disappears. By the time

Carol has finished with her, visibly disappointed at not being allowed to "do something" with her long hair, a nameless boy is waiting to escort her to the studio.

'Come back later and I'll remove your make-up,' says Carol. 'Most people don't want to walk out with the make-up on and I'll be here.'

'Follow me, bring your bag,' says the boy impatiently and walks ahead of her down a long corridor into the actual studio. 'You can put you bag on the shelf here.'

The set is a bright circular island of colour floating in a barely lit space of grey floor and dark pieces of equipment. She knew that it would just be a small stage with furniture and background props in an empty room, but she is surprised at how big the studio is, with cameras and cables snaking across the floor and two men with earphones doing unexplained things. The set is stylish and minimalistic with three orange armchairs in a semi-circle and a low table like a shiny yellow drum in front of them. There are glasses and a carafe of water on the table and in the centre a bowl with red gerberas and trailing greenery, that makes Callista think of tentacles.

They step up on the raised platform that forms the floor of the set, and the young man says, 'Are you going to wear the jacket during the interview, or do you want to take it off now? I need to know how to mic you.'

Callista says she wants to keep the jacket on, and he inserts a microphone cable up the back of her jacket and asks her to grab it and pull it under her arm and clip it to the front edge beside the buttons. He points at the chair at the end of the semi-circle and smiles, suddenly relaxed and cheerful looking. 'You can sit down now, you're all ready to go. Any questions?'

Chapter 13

The cameras move slightly and one of the dimly visible cameramen calls out, 'Could you look over here, please?' and waves his arm and then strong lights come on and she can no longer see the cameras, but she knows where they are; their little red dots of light penetrate the glare from the spotlights. The man from the make-up room comes in and sits down in the chair beside Callista, followed by Ronald who takes the chair at the far end of the little semi-circle, facing her. She wonders why she is not next to him, if she is to be interviewed first, and her apprehension increases.

Why did Ronald not introduce the man who now sits less than a metre from her? Is he the guest after her, is he just sitting there without a voice until her interview is finished, or is he someone who saw the incident in Salcombe and can describe it? Has he provided video of it? Were they kept apart on purpose to prevent them talking to each other? Will they spring a video she has never seen on her, unannounced while on live TV? Her mind is swirling with apprehension and potentially disastrous theories. The seeming deviousness of this situation and the helpless feeling of uncertainty make her nervous, which is probably exactly why they did it this way. If they can get her off balance she might provide 'better TV', maybe lose her temper, say something revealing or cry. Inside she shudders at their tactics and steels herself to keep calm, to not allow knee-jerk reactions to take over from reasoned responses.

Someone she cannot see counts down loudly from the dark space and then it's on; Ronald greets the viewers, outlines the program content and turns to Callista.

'Callista Bannister, welcome!' he says smiling and friendly looking, but still without introducing the second guest. 'I'm so pleased you could join us. You are flavour of the month everywhere now, and we are all fascinated by what happened at Okehampton. I appreciate you coming in to talk about it! Let's start by playing that video of your amazing experience that I'm sure we've all watched more than once.'

. . .

Callista watches the video on the screen behind Ronald and wonders if there is another screen behind her where he can see it, a screen positioned where her face and the screen will show in the same shot, so viewers can see her reactions. She tries to watch without displaying any emotion, while inside she desperately hopes that there will be no surprises.

When the recording ends Ronald says, in a concerned and caring voice belied by the expression in his eyes that seems to indicate excitement, 'As we saw just now, this premonition or communication that you experienced caused you distress, maybe physical pain. Can you describe what it was, what it felt like?'

'I don't know what it was or what caused it.' Callista moves her head slowly from side to side, the way people do when they are baffled, the way she checked in the mirror last night and decided would be a good gesture to go with her declaration of confused innocence. 'It was just a powerful feeling that he had a weapon and was going to kill someone – I truly felt certain that he was going to pull out a gun and shoot someone. And the only person I could see anywhere near me was the man standing about ten metres in front of me.'

'How did it feel? In the video you're holding your hands to your head the way people do when they feel a stabbing pain.'

'Oh yes, I did feel pain – quite intense - but just for a moment and I felt dizzy.'

'But how could you be so sure which person this warning came from? The gun was out of sight under his jacket – I believe he had a holster strapped to his torso with the gun under his left armpit, and he had his back to you. Some people have suggested you knew this ahead of time, that you had some advance knowledge.' He smiles. 'I'm not suggesting that you did, but the idea has been circulated on the internet.'

This angle is one she has predicted; she knows the reputation this program has for suddenly trying to pin their guests to the wall in the middle of a seemingly innocent interview, and she has tried to prepare herself for everything they might throw at her.

'No, I'd never seen him before. I'm not sure if you know this, but the police have interviewed at least a dozen people, who can vouch for it that I arrived long after him, and that he was already out there at the top of the hill before I even arrived at the parking area.

'But what I wonder – and I'm sure we all do,' says Ronald, giving all the appearance of a genuinely puzzled and concerned man, 'is how did you know the message, if we can all it that, came from him?'

'I have no idea. But I had no doubt that it was from him – not for a moment. When I had this thought that he was going to kill someone, I looked in the direction his head was turned - he was looking slightly to the left, and I saw that a little group of children had appeared at the bottom of the hill and were starting the climb up towards us. I hadn't noticed them until that moment, but it never occurred to me that there was anyone but that man who was a threat.'

Ronald decides to leave the subject and tries another angle. 'That couple who approached you, who came running up from behind you - they thought you were ill. How did they react when you told them he had a gun?'

Callista looks at him, still with the half a smile that she has practiced in the mirror until she can produce it without effort, and says with the appearance of total calm, 'They reacted in exactly the same way I would have in the same situation. Of course, they didn't believe it, nobody in their right mind would - they thought I was mad.'

Ronald blinks, just for a moment he is visibly caught by surprise, which Callista observes with pleasure, but hopefully with a straight face. She senses a tiny movement beside her and slides a sideways glance at the unnamed man and sees the corner of his mouth twitch.

'And you were so sure of his intentions that you were prepared to tackle him, a man you felt certain was armed – and dangerous? You thought that was the only option you had?' Ronald has recovered his poise and is once again in charge of the conversation.

She looks steadily at him for a long silent moment, and she can tell that she is not what he expected, he is revising his opinion and possibly his strategy.

'Ronald, I think you must agree that the video we just watched shows that tackling him *was* in fact the only option, the only way to prevent a tragedy. I think it's completely irrelevant what I thought or didn't think at that moment - he really *did* have a gun and by the time I reached him he had pulled it out and had it in his hand - and the children were climbing up the slope towards him. And nobody else was doing anything about it.'

She moves her gaze to the red dot where a camera is placed just to one side of and behind Ronald's shoulder. She is prepared to bet it is filming an ultra-close-up of her face, and she says in a conversational tone of voice, as if she's talking to the camera and the viewers. 'I didn't invite this to happen to me, you know - it was a horrible experience, painful and frightening, but someone had to do something.'

She hears a low chuckle from the man beside her, slides another glance in his direction, meets his eyes briefly and feels a ripple of warmth, like a light touch. Whoever he is, he is enjoying this understated duel between Ronald and herself and it gives her confidence.

Ronald recovers his wits and moves to stop any

further attempts of hers to take over his show by turning abruptly to the man between them.

'And with us tonight we also have Cosmo St Clair, scientist and well-known commentator on psychic claims and other beliefs and rumours not backed by scientific evidence. Cosmo is the spokesman for the group commonly referred to as 'the sceptics', but their proper name is Sceptics in Science. Interesting initials, by the way! What's your take on this, Cosmo?'

'I don't believe in ESP, as you know, Ronald,' says Cosmo. 'And I'm not saying this didn't happen, because obviously it did - but I don't believe it happened due to ESP. The fact that it happened does not prove that some psychic phenomenon took place.'

'But how do you explain it?'

'I don't − it's not up to me to explain it. I don't understand it, but until all other possibilities have been eliminated, I don't accept it as proof of ESP, to use the common term.'

'What do you think of Cosmo's attitude, Callista? Does it upset you to hear someone dismiss this event as not ESP?'

'No, of course not,' she says with a little laugh that seems to come quite naturally. She is determined not to play into his hands and without thinking she knows she must give the appearance of finding his questions and innuendo slightly ridiculous. 'I don't believe in ESP either. I can only paraphrase Mr. StClair's words - I don't know *how* it happened or why – but it *did* happen.'

She feels some kind of vibe coming from St Clair and turns her head; he is looking directly at her now and he looks puzzled. As well you might, she thinks, I bet you thought I would leap on the chance of those fifteen minutes of fame that Patrick was going on about. You thought I would grab this opportunity with both hands and make the most of it, ramble on about my unique talent or some other rubbish.

'And how have your parents reacted to this?' Ronald's face once again wears its mask of well-rehearsed concern. 'Are they worried about you? After the accident in Salcombe last year, it must have been a shock that you had yet another ... experience.'

Callista's mind produces a split-second reaction when he utters the word 'accident'; she knows without a doubt that the next words are going to be "in Salcombe" - and she knows that this is the moment she has been waiting for, the reason she agreed to be on the show. Now she can use some of the phrases she has thought up beforehand, try to play down what happened in Salcombe, diminish her role. What she fears most is that there will be a video of that event too, in which case she will have no options left.

'Of course, my parents are worried,' she says, trying to keep her voice easy and natural. 'They know that having reporters and cameras on my doorstep is irritating and sometimes it feels like an intrusion into my privacy - it's not easy to live with that uninvited scrutiny. But you are not *quite* right about Salcombe. I didn't actually have an accident.' She hopes her face looks calmer than she feels. 'I only *very nearly* had an accident. A car crashed into a shop window just in front of me, but I wasn't hit, not like some more unfortunate people were, they are the ones who deserve sympathy and attention – there were some serious injuries, but I only got a small cut on my arm from a flying piece of glass. I was more a bystander than anything else.'

Ever since she received the anonymous text message, she has been rehearsing what she will say to anyone who brings this up in public. The only way to distance herself from speculation is to defuse the drama aspect, to try to remove herself from any direct involvement.

'A very dramatic incident, if what I've heard is true.' He looks enquiringly at her, clearly indicating that he expects an answer, but she waits, says nothing and continues to look at him in what she hopes is an unconcerned way.

If he wants an answer, he will have to re-phrase it as a question, she thinks. He knows something and he expects to be able to get a reaction out of me, but maybe I can ride this out by just waiting, though it is nerve wracking. She can imagine what his tactics are, he will get her to elaborate a bit and then he'll hook on to something she says and ask yet another question, and then it would be like unravelling knitting by pulling on a loose end of wool. She feels certain that he knows more than he has let on, and she wonders why he is holding back at all. To reveal more now in a live broadcast would be a huge scoop for the program; something they can put on social media that will be shared thousands of times and increase the program's ratings.

Cosmo St Clair intervenes casually, as if this has been a three-way conversation from the start. 'I imagine that having a crash happen that close to you would be terrifying. And you weren't injured at all - apart from that cut?'

Intensely grateful to him for this bland intervention that takes the pressure off her for a moment, she turns sideways in her chair to face him, excludes Ronald from the conversation and says, 'Yes, it was scary - and it happened so quickly. The car came towards me really fast and I kind of leapt to the side and I fell, mostly from fright or surprise, I think, not because I was hit. I had a feeling afterwards that I knocked a couple of people over when I flung myself to the side. But apart from that cut on my arm I wasn't hurt at all.'

Cosmo smiles and shakes his head, as in disbelief. 'Very lucky!'

· · ·

The interview ends a couple of minutes later, after some in Callista's opinion, excessive raving from Ronald about her sprint and how she tackled the man at Okehampton. They replay the end of the video, from the point where she started running towards the man to the point where she kicked the gun out of his hand, but Callista doesn't watch it. She looks down at the flower arrangement on the table and counts backward by threes from ninety-nine until it is over.

Chapter 14

Callista unclips the microphone, slides the cable out from under her jacket and says a casual 'Thank you!' to Ronald, who thanks her for coming and turns immediately to speak to St Clair. She knows she has been dismissed, she can feel his still simmering annoyance at the way she side-lined him, but she is deeply thankful that both men are staying on the set during the ad break. She negotiates the cables on the floor, picks up her bag from the shelf by the door and walks out of the studio with a feeling of release, lighter, as if something has been lifted from her. Hesitating for only a moment she makes a snap decision not to take up the offer of having her make-up removed.

. . .

What she needs to do now, is get away from these people who regard her as a temporary asset, someone to be manipulated to enhance their ratings, and she knows where she will take refuge and be alone for a few quiet minutes. There is nobody at the reception desk, but the big glass door is unlocked, and she leaves the TV company's premises and turns left towards the toilets that she saw signposted when she came up the emergency stairs from the ground floor lobby.

The interview has made her feel as if she has been on trial, under the guise of concern and interest. So cleverly done, she thinks, and so devious. And did the watching public get the impression that I am somehow a suspect? Do they now look at me as a possible fraud or a collaborator of the gun man? Or has it just reinforced the opinion of many that I have some supernatural power? I can't see it from their point of view, and people will have different opinions, but the feeling that sits at the top of my mind is that I was on trial, suspected or accused of an unnamed crime.

She stands in front of the basin and slowly washes her hands while she tries to identify the factors that have made her feel so unsettled. It wasn't just the way Ronald phrased things to draw things out of me and tried to trick me - I had expected that, it's his job and I had my answers prepared. But the way he made that deliberate pause before the word 'experience', when he talked about Salcombe, that felt like a threat. As if he were indicating he knew something, that he could suddenly bring something out to take me by surprise. I had to be so careful, because I didn't know what would come next, maybe a video or a witness. He made me feel as if I were a criminal or a liar. And the way he didn't introduce Cosmo in the make-up room and obviously took him off somewhere until right at the start, that was a tactic meant to unbalance me and make me feel vulnerable. For all I knew, he could have been someone who witnessed the Salcombe crash or maybe filmed it.

She dries her hands and remains where she is, looking at herself in the mirror and feels exhausted and empty, nearly damaged.

She was not prepared for how intense this would be, not to this extent; being put on display and then played like a fish on a line – or rather he tried to play her, but she doesn't think his plan came off quite the way he expected it to. She could tell he was revising his opinion of what type of person she is right from the start. But she hadn't realised how hard it would be to keep her cool in that situation, or how much concentration it would take to keep her face hopefully looking bland and unconcerned, while talking or listening – and the whole time, thoughts were streaming through her head. She had felt the undercurrent coming from him the whole time, his feigned interest a cover for something, but he held back, and she still doesn't know what it was, or why he didn't bring it up. She thinks he must have heard a bit more about Salcombe, but he has no direct evidence yet, so he thought he would taunt her and see if she would rise to the bait. But his nearly invisible fury when she refused to answer his non-question and nearly took the lead role away from him and talked directly to the camera! She doubts that anyone will understand how strongly she could feel his lust for revenge after that and how hard it was to keep calm. The thing that made her feel stronger was that phrase that popped into her head while she sat silently waiting for him to continue; "oh, sorry – was that a question? I thought you just made a statement." It had made her feel that she had one more line of defence if he challenged her.

She looks unseeing at her image in the mirror and thinks, he emailed what he wanted to talk about, but he was unprepared for my answers, so I think I won on points, but I totally overestimated my ability to cope with this. I must get better at surviving these ordeals or just refuse to take part in, or listen to, any further media debates about this. The reality of it was so much worse than I had expected it to be – sitting in that huge dark space, in a bubble of bright light with crew people you can't see watching from the shadows and the big audience at home in their living rooms hoping for drama. The only thing I wanted to achieve with this was to have a chance at a pre-emptive strike before the Salcombe incident becomes topic of the day, and I think I have done that reasonably well.

Using wet paper towels and liquid soap she scrubs the make-up off her skin and studies the result. Her face looks blotchy, but she knows it will soon fade and rather than trying to use soap to remove the heavy mascara, she leaves it on as a better option than having panda eyes on the bus trip home. Outside the toilets she stands undecisive for a minute and tries to make up her mind which way to go, but in the end, she heads towards the lift.

That man, Cosmo, he has something which I've never come across before, and I don't understand what it is. There is a feeling around him that affects me, but I'm not sure what it is. And that slight amusement that he tried to conceal, that was unsettling too. Probably he was hiding a smirk, thinking that I was an attention grabber - but why he would think that, I can't imagine, not after the sort of things I said in response to Ronald. Or was that smirk before I had kind of drawn my line in the sand? I can't remember. And why would he then be kind enough to create that little diversion at the end, to take the pressure off me? Such conflicting messages, it makes me wonder if I can read people's emotions and motives at all. And what is that thing that radiates out from him, I've never before felt anything like that coming from another human being, not ever.

Callista crosses the landing to the lift, presses the Down button and waits. She is grateful that she is not going to share the lift with anyone, this is the first time since she was a young teenager that she has used one, and she is taking a calculated risk, but the thought of going down all those flights of semi-dark emergency stairs just now, when she is feeling slightly off-kilter already, is too much. She acknowledges to herself that this is not her usual reaction to either darkness or being alone, but tonight she is off balance and six flights of echoing, badly lit stairs are not for her; a few seconds in a lift seems more manageable just now. Just as the lift door opens, she hears rapid footsteps behind her and turns to see Cosmo St Clair coming towards her.

'Thanks!' he says, as she holds a hand over the edge of the lift door to stop it shutting in his face. 'The time it took to get all that gunk off my face!'

She makes no reply and then, within seconds of starting its descent the lift stops, the lights flicker and go out and the silence and darkness feel like a threat, something that might harm her and her heartbeat speeds up.

This can't be happening, she thinks, I must not panic! I can't lose control, not with him in here, this is a nightmare! I must be calm - I can't let panic take over!

To take the risk and try to hold herself together for fifteen or twenty seconds in the lift going down was one thing, being stuck and unable to get out of this small, enclosed space is something totally different. The fear is so powerful that she cannot use reason to dispel it, she clenches her fists and leans into the back corner, tries to control her panting breaths and tells herself over and over that she is safe, there is nothing here that can harm her, she is safe; the mantra she has been taught to use when claustrophobia grips her. Her inner self curls into a hard mass in her chest, and she knows that she is going to die.

Chapter 15

Cosmo turns his cellphone on, holds it up and uses its light to study the panel, while Callista stands as if frozen with her teeth clamped together to prevent a moan of desperation escaping

'What the hell? Is there one of those call buttons?' he says quietly, as if to himself, and she watches his finger press the Help button repeatedly, but nothing happens. He bends down and talks into the little grill beside the button, 'Hello! Can you hear me?' but there is no response.

'Well, that's it then. I'll see what I can find out on the internet – let's hope I've got reception in here.'

His fingers move over the screen on his phone, but Callista pays no attention; her entire focus now is on controlling the urge to scream and start clawing at the door. The 'I am safe, there is no danger' mantra is not working, somewhere in some distant corner of her brain she knows, even while she tries to concentrate on diminishing her fear, that this is a worse situation that any she has been in for many years, perhaps ever. Cosmo has turned away from the panel and is facing her; his face lit vaguely by the light from his phone as he searches the internet.

'Total blackout in half of Devon and part of Somerset, but I've found a phone number,' he says and puts the phone to his ear.

Callista pushes her fingernails hard into the palms of her hands and the pain helps, shifts her focus and makes her feel marginally less on the verge of total melt-down.

'No, that's all right,' says Cosmo to someone, sounding quite relaxed. 'No, there are two of us. No, I understand that, of course you can't – we can wait.'

He listens for a moment and then he chuckles, 'No, we're not about to go into labour and we don't have chest pains. OK, thanks!'

He ends the call, and the light from the screen goes off. 'They can't come for about an hour – we'll have to wait until some urgent situations have been dealt with first. Or if the power comes back on, the lift might just start up again. He said it should, but sometimes the only way to get it going again is to re-boot it manually.'

Callista says, in a reedy voice, 'I'll sit on the floor and wait.'

'Good idea.'

She's not going to talk to me, he thinks, and feels his way to the rear corner on what he now thinks of as his side of the lift and sits down. She sounds as if she would rather be anywhere than in this lift with me. She probably thinks I'm her enemy and she can't bear to talk to me, pity – I'd like to have a proper conversation about whatever she thinks this so-called ability of hers is all about, but I don't think that's going to happen. There were some things she said that intrigued me and I thought we had some kind of rapport during the interview, but I can tell she'd probably rather talk to Ronald than to me. How typical that this happened in this old-fashioned narrow lift, enforced proximity – she'll just have to put up with me being quite close.

He gets his phone out again and opens the book he is reading on his Kobo app, but within a couple of minutes something alerts him, a feeling that something is deeply wrong. He tilts the phone at an angle and shines its light into the other corner. Callista is leaning sideways against the wall, her eyes are shut and a single tear trickles slowly down the cheek he can see, and then another tear wells out from under long eyelashes. Silently he studies her pale face for a few moments; her breathing is rapid and shallow, her hands are clenched into fists, resting on her thighs.

Christ! he thinks, she's scared out of her mind, terrified. He turns the phone away from her and considers what to do, but short of breaking the door open, which isn't an option, the only thing he can do is try his best to calm her down. Not that I've ever had to deal with this sort of thing before, but how hard can it be? Maybe it's the same as trying to settle Dessi when she wakes up from a nightmare, just a calm voice and lots of patience, just being there.

He puts the phone in his pocket and moves over until he is next to her. 'Don't worry, we'll be OK – we've just got to wait until the lift guy gets here or the power comes on.'

She hears him, but his words don't register in her mind where uncontrollable panic is so close to get away from her that replying is beyond her. Her entire concentration must stay focused on retaining her precarious grip on her fear, not to let it get away from her and turn her into a sobbing wreck, clawing at the walls. In her head the same thought returns over and over again, 'I'm going to die'. She turns her head further into the wall, tries to hide as much of herself as she can. She knows that she is going to die, that any second now her heart will stop.

. . .

Half turning towards her Cosmo reaches out and takes the hand closest to him and holds it, still fisted, in his. Her hand is cold, and the arm is stiff and unwilling to move even that small distance, but he rests their joined hands on his thigh and moves his thumb slowly back and forth over her wrist.

'We'll be out of here soon, there's no danger – the lift isn't going to drop, we just have to wait, we're perfectly safe.'

They sit like that for a minute while Cosmo tries to think of something else to say to take her mind off the situation. If it were Dessi, I'd tell her a story she likes, but heaven knows what kind of story this girl would listen to. I don't think The Tiger Who Came to Tea is going to work here.

She leans into the wall away from him; her breaths are still shallow and panting. He is just about to make a comment about the possible cause for the blackout, which seems like an unthreatening subject, when he realises that his hand feels sticky. He gets the phone out and turns it on, shines it briefly on the side of their joined hands and sees blood. Shit! She's so scared that she's cut her palm open with her nails, this is serious fear, panic. He returns the phone to his pocket and moves closer.

. . .

Callista hears his movements and feels him close beside her, but only as something on the periphery of her consciousness, inside her mind she battles desperation and the urge to flee, and the effort to stave off screaming panic uses all her mental strength leaving nothing for speculation about what he is doing. Cosmo lets her hand go, leans closer and takes hold of her shoulders; he pulls her close at the same time as he moves himself over to cover the remaining few inches between them. He turns her and holds her tight against his chest with one arm around her back, the other hand anchoring her head against his shoulder.

In Callista's head conflicting urges nearly overwhelm her. She wants to pull away, to hide, but she cannot speak.

'Shush,' he says, using the words he says to Dessi when she wakes up frightened in the night. 'It's OK now, I've got you. Nothing is going to happen to you. I'm here, I've got you.'

He moves his hand from the back of her head and picks up her hand that is caught between their bodies. Gently he unclenches her fist and curls his fingers around hers, feels the stickiness of blood and thinks, claustrophobia, that's what it is. She's terrified of being locked in, paralyzed by fear. Why on earth did she get into the lift in the first place? And what can I do? I can't open the doors and we might be between floors anyway, and I don't know what you're supposed to do with someone in this state. He leans his cheek against the top of her head and continues to quietly mumble meaningless phrases of reassurance and suddenly her body relaxes as if her bones have melted. She goes limp and rests her weight against him, her head slides forward, the hand he is holding unfurls and she sighs.

In Callista's mind layers of terror peel away, leaving a dim, white space of calm and silence. 'I'm sorry,' she says quietly. 'I panicked.'

'I know, you're claustrophobic, aren't you?'

'Yes,' is all she says, and she knows she should move away, but she so tired now and reluctant to move away from the safety of this body that somehow seems able to shield her from her fear. Everything that has happened tonight has been an endurance test: being prepared, keeping control of her expression, not letting herself be trapped into saying something she doesn't want to, seeming cool and reasonable in the face of manipulation and deviousness and all of this live with thousands watching, and the final assault, being locked in a stalled lift. She closes her eyes and within a minute she is asleep.

Cosmo moves slowly sideways in small increments and moves Callista with him until he is leaning into the corner. He pulls his knees up and creates a space where Callista is secured by his thighs on one side and his chest on the other, leans his head against the wall and closes his eyes.

An hour and half later the light comes on with blinding suddenness and a second later the machinery starts up; the lift makes a jump and continues its journey to the ground floor. Callista opens her eyes and realises that Cosmo is holding her and that she has been asleep. Gently he sets her upright and they get to their feet, but she can think of nothing to say. It is too confusing, too strange and she hesitates to meet his eyes. When the door slides open, she doesn't move, and he picks up her bag and hands it to her. Slowly she reaches for the bag, and he takes her hand. 'Come on, time to go home.'

They walk across the brightly lit foyer to the glass doors, where she can see traffic moving and streetlights on. Everything is back to normal, and it seems strange that the world has casually continued its business, albeit in the dark, while she went through something so cataclysmic. When he reaches out to push open the glass door, she sees blood on his hand and feels herself blushing.

'I am so sorry!' she says again, hangs the strap of the bag over her shoulder and looks down at her own hands. 'I didn't know I had done that.'

'Of course, you didn't,' he says calmly and gestures for her to go ahead of him. 'Do you want a ride home?'

'I'll walk thanks.' She is so embarrassed and confused, that the thought of getting into a car with him seems impossible, but he doesn't leave, he stands there looking at her with a thoughtful expression, as if he is working something out.

'I don't think that's a good idea. You've been through a terrible ordeal and it's late. Come along!'

And for some reason she can't understand, she walks beside him to his car, gets in and sits silent as he starts the engine and turns to look at her. 'Where do you live?'

'I live in Exeter – can you drop me at the bus station, please?'

Chapter 16

After a brief silence he looks searchingly at her and says, 'It's probably too late for a bus now, it's nearly quarter to eleven.'

'It can't be! I was only asleep for a few minutes.' She can make no sense of what he just said, and it adds to her confusion about the situation she is in. Twice before she has fallen asleep after a particularly bad episode of claustrophobia, but never for more than a few minutes.

'It was a bit longer than that,' he says gently, trying to minimize the impact which he feels sure is going to embarrass her.

The realisation that he did not just hold her for a few minutes, but she slept deeply for well over an hour while he sat patiently holding her, makes her feel deeply troubled. The man who, she had decided, thought she

138

was a flaky attention seeker or maybe a bit mad, has not only talked her out of a panic, but he looked after her as if she was his sister or his child. She blocks the word lover as inappropriate, seeing who they are; two people thrown together by chance, basically on opposite sides of a very high fence and probably with little in common. Get your act together, she chides herself, don't sit here looking like a dimwit, say something.

'Thank you,' she says without quite meeting his eyes. 'You've been very kind – and patient.'

He makes no response to this, just says, as if unaware of her embarrassment, 'I live just outside Tedburn St Mary, so it's not far out of my way. I thought you had a car – I saw it in that photo from the Okehampton car park. Why did you come on the bus?'

'The battery is flat – I thought I had charged it enough by driving around, but it might be something worse. I took the bus instead.' And then she adds, 'I thought you lived in London - I've heard you on radio quite a lot lately and I got the impression that's where you live.'

She is sure he knows that she is thinking of all the times in the past week that he has been asked for his opinion about what happened at Okehampton, and his unflinching stance of scepticism and disbelief.

'I'm in London quite often, but I've always lived in Tedburn, I'm still in the house where I grew up.'

They drive in silence through the late evening traffic, out of the centre of Plymouth and towards Tavistock.

'Do you go this way to Exeter? Right around Dartmoor?' she says, forgetting how embarrassed and awkward she felt only ten minutes ago. 'I always take the road to the south, it's quicker.'

'Sometimes I go this way,' is all he says, and she leans her head back and nearly falls asleep again; her eyes keep closing and she drifts off into short snatches of sleep until she wakes up fully with a start of alarm.

'Where are we? What are you doing?' She is annoyed to hear how anxious her voice sounds.

'Just turning into Castle Lane in Okehampton - there's something I want us to look at together.'

She sits up straight and turns to stare at him. 'Why? I don't want to go here and it's dark, we can't see anything - please turn around!'

'Bear with me for just a few minutes. I want to be here with you, to stand where you stood and try to understand – something. I'm not sure what, but I think this is a good opportunity. There won't be anyone else here this late at night. And don't worry, I won't let anything happen to you, I'll be right beside you the whole time.'

They are at the parking area now, and he turns the engine off and opens his door, but she stays where she is and thinks that he simply doesn't understand, and she probably won't be able to explain to him that this is not something anyone can protect her from.

'No! Whatever this is, you can't protect me from it – *nobody* can. It just comes! You wouldn't even know it was happening, nobody else notices until it's too late, until it's in my head. And it's awful!'

This is one step too far, it's going to tip her over the edge into something she simply can't deal with, she's had enough for one day. Ever since her visit here, she has wondered if Salcombe was the first step and what happened here was the second, leading to some final outcome that she can't bear to contemplate, some form of mental illness or breakdown, her mind being taken over, never to be given back. She has no fear of the castle ruins themselves, but she dreads the thought that standing where she stood that day will bring back a memory so strong that it will overwhelm her with pain and terror, just like the actual event nearly did.

He is on her side of the car now, he opens the door and reaches in to open the glove compartment, pulls something out and crouches down beside her. Looking down she sees that he is holding a packet of wet wipes; he takes her unresisting hands, one after the other, and wipes the dried blood away very gently, pats the wounds on her palms and throws the tissues on the floor at her feet, then he gets up and wipes her dried blood off his own hands. In the open glove compartment lie three small parcels wrapped in tissues and tied inexpertly with string, a pink and yellow plastic unicorn and a silver whistle with a blue ribbon tied to it.

'I know what happened up there was frightening,' he says and studies her reluctant face. 'I know it made you feel terrible. But I did manage to help you out of that claustrophobic episode in the lift.'

He hopes he is right, that it was what he did that broke the spell of her fear, and that she won't resent him for mentioning it. 'I think I *can* protect you and keep you safe - but you have to trust me. You think we are enemies, don't you? You think that I dislike you or perhaps you think I despise you – but I don't, I never did. I just dispute the notion that what happened to you is your mind channelling someone else's thoughts. I respect you, Callista - you are so brave and calm about this extraordinary experience you've had. And the claustrophobia has nothing to do with it, does it?'

'No – I've had it all my life. But I really don't want to go up there tonight – please let's not!'

She can't tell him of her fear that going back will kindle memories so strong that she might be unable to cope; that today is too soon. But he hunkers down beside her again and takes one of her cold hands in his warm one.

'Callista, listen to me – I think it's important for you

to dispel the idea that going up there will bring something back, something you won't be able to handle – whether it's a memory or something else. If we stand together where you stood, you might be able to explain it to me – to describe exactly what happened and something might come back to you, something important about how this works, and I really want to know. And if nothing ... invasive happens, at least you will know that it was the time and the person that caused it, not the place.'

Does he really mean it? She is unsure of his motives despite his stated desire to just understand what happened. But as she looks into his face, she sees no sarcasm or scorn, none of the things she has suspected him of.

'I did think you despised me, that you thought I'm ridiculous - or maybe just attention seeking.'

'No, of course not, I never thought any of those things. We're probably more alike than you think, in fact I feel sure we are. Right now, I just want to try and understand this from a rational point of view – instead of the mystical and sensational angle that the media take, which I think is harmful, not only to you, but to the general public. My disbelief is not about you, it's about the interpretation everyone is applying to the phenomenon itself.'

. . .

He lets go of her hand, gets to his feet and stands silently looking down at her, so she gets out of the car, and they walk across the road in near darkness with the stars the only source of light. They climb the rough grass slope to the first line of stone walls, where the higher remnants of the castle show dimly as dark shapes against the star-bright night sky.

'Further along, I remember which part of the ruins was straight behind you, it's in that other video that hardly anybody shared, the one someone took from below and to one side,' says Cosmo and they walk a few steps along the outer wall until he is satisfied that they are in the right place.

From up here they can see the lights from Okehampton village some way distant, a few houses with lights still on and streetlights, and Callista looks down the slope and shakes her head. 'I was further down when I heard that … voice. Just a little bit further down.'

'Stop here,' he says and gets his phone out. 'Let's check it, we can't be far off – we can look at the other video and orientate ourselves.'

He holds his phone and watches the screen, and they walk forward a few steps. 'Stop - I think this is pretty close to where you stood. In the video a couple more houses down there show beside those trees, but we can't see them because we're lower than the guy who held the camera.'

Callista looks down and to both sides, imagines the scene in daylight, studies the outlines of the clumps of trees, the paler area where a stretch of the road shows and identifies the spot where the cluster of children stood when she first noticed them.

'Yes, this is it,' she says quietly and suppresses an urge to reach out and take his hand. She knows they are probably within a few feet of where she was when those thoughts invaded her mind. She stares straight ahead at the spot where the gun man stood that day, as if she should still be able to see his back, but absolutely nothing occurs to her, no hint of fear or premonition, no painful intrusion in her mind, and no reaction to the memory.

She looks down again to the bottom of the hill where the children started their climb. She remembers them laughing and calling out to each other, and how terrified she was on their behalf, fearing she would see some of them fall, injured or dead, hear them screaming with fear, covered in blood. She pictures what she noticed as she ran towards the man; his right elbow angled out as he bent his arm to get the gun out from inside his jacket when she was a couple steps short of him. She imagines the feel of how she launched herself, her shoulder slamming into his back with her full weight behind it and they toppled; he crashed forward onto his knees, nearly over-balanced, and she rolled half over him, half to one side. In her mind she can feel herself twisting as she landed and seeing the gun in his hand, and then the two boys throwing themselves at the man and a shot going off. She hears in her mind the grunts of the men struggling and visualizes herself getting to her feet and kicking the man's hand and how the gun flew in an arc through the air and landed further down the slope. She recreates the entire scene in her mind, and nothing happens.

'Nothing,' she says, deeply relieved. 'I feel nothing at all. I know I was reluctant to come here in case the memory of it would be too much after - everything. But the memory is just a memory - very vivid, very detailed, but it's not taking over my mind.'

She turns to look at him, she can't make out his expression, but she feels an intense need to explain, to make him understand precisely what it was that happened.

'You must listen to me, Cosmo - I need to tell you how it was, how it felt. I've been certain all along that what I heard in my head that day was coming straight from him, that it was his thoughts in real time. He thought "I'll pull the gun out now and shoot some of those children" - it was as if he spoke inside my head at the very moment the thought formed in his head. I felt as if I heard something, but the voice left no impression, I can't describe it by accent or timbre. But they were spoken words, definitely spoken words, it wasn't just a thought – much more clearly defined, more deliberate.'

'You haven't said that in pubic before – that it was a voice and spoken words. You've said that it was as clear as if he stood next to you, but that's all. Was that really what you experienced, a voice speaking, did you feel that at the time or is it a way of describing how you knew it was a man.'

She shakes her head and thinks how odd this is, how unexpected, that she finds herself prepared to tell him what only one or two people know, the fact that she so carefully didn't mention when talking to Ronald.

'No, it's how it was – a voice, spoken words, without any doubt a man's voice. I deliberately haven't said that in public, not in so many words, because I'm worried it will make me sound even crazier. Hearing voices! They'd lock me up.'

Something in the change of tone makes him try to see her face more clearly, but the darkness hides her expression. He takes a step closer. 'Are you worried that there is something wrong with your brain?'

She remains silent and he pauses before he continues. 'It's not for me to question you, and I can understand how you might worry about it, but I'm sure it's not some anomaly in your brain – I think it was something that came to you from outside you.'

And then he laughs, genuinely surprised and amused. 'Did I really say that? I think I just admitted that it's some kind of thought transfer thing – I might have to stop being a rationalist, I've blown my credibility.'

And she smiles in the darkness, because she thought exactly the same thing when she heard that comforting comment "something that comes to you from outside you".

'But thank you!' says Cosmo now, very aware of how he coaxed her into coming here, insisted that they try this experiment and how frightened she had been. 'I hoped some additional detail might surface that would help explain things. I've never doubted that you were telling the exact truth - you are very rational and analytical and honest. I just hoped to gain some additional insight. I'm sorry I made you do this, but it might have worked.'

'It's OK, don't worry about it. And it was good that I did it, at least now I know that coming here won't bring on some kind of flash-back. And it *did* work – it changed your mind.'

She hesitates for a moment, but the need to reinforce her message wins, and she continues, stays where she is, facing him in the dark.

'I've told you this already, but I must make sure you really understand this – I know without a doubt that I heard his thoughts like spoken words or how would I have known to do what I did? I saw his elbow bend as I ran towards him – as he reached inside his jacket with his right hand to pull the gun out. And even as I ran so fast and felt so energized and so angry – even *then* I thought "I *was* right, he *is* doing it" – as if I wanted to document it, to justify my warning that those people didn't believe. Do you understand what I'm telling you?'

This is the first time she has gone into so much detail, and somehow it is important to make sure he understands what it was like being the one in whose mind those word appeared from nowhere, so that he really understands how it felt. She can't see his expression and takes a step closer. 'Do you understand what it was like now?'

'Oh yes, I do, completely. I can't explain it and I don't understand how it works, but I can relive it through you.' He grips her shoulders and holds her firmly and she feels the warmth of his hands through her jacket. 'Do you feel frightened now? Does the place itself make you feel uneasy?'

She knows what he is getting at, he still underestimates her to some degree, and it amuses her, and she smiles in the dark. 'No, I'm not frightened - I have no superstitious fear of this place. I didn't get myself into a state, as they call it – the vibes of this place didn't make me imagine things. It was *him*, not the place. The ruins are just that - ruins of something long gone, they can't influence my mind.'

He lets her go, but stays where he is, only a step

away. 'You're extremely good at describing things - thank you for sharing all these details. And you're right, it did happen, and you did have advance knowledge of what he was about to do – you could never have randomly guessed it as some have suggested, the odds against it are astronomical. I hope you understand that what drives me is an urge to come to grips with this, because it is one of the very few times something like this has happened and been documented and witnessed in real time, not just re-told afterwards. I think it is the best documented event of its kind anywhere – that video is amazing.'

'I know, but I still can't explain what it was or how it works,' she says sadly. 'I wish I could. It arrived uninvited and involved me in something that in retrospect terrifies me. The thought that I might not have reacted fast enough, failed to prevent him killing one or more of those children. It is such a responsibility. And why me – would it have involved another person, if they had happened to stand exactly where I was in relation to him at that exact moment? Was this due to proximity and some kind of mental link that got amplified randomly and let my mind hear what was in his?'

Chapter 17

Walking down the slope is far more difficult than climbing up was. Below them the clumps of trees look very dark, and they are not looking up towards the starlit sky as they were on the way up; they are walking away from the light instead of towards it.

'Careful - don't trip!' he says from behind her when she stumbles. 'You know, you have a fantastic kick – the way you kicked his hand with the side of your foot and sent the gun flying – great aim.'

'I played football right through school and university, and I was pretty good at it, so I've had lots of practice.'

She hears his deep chuckle behind her. 'I was just about to suggest you should take up football – you read my mind.'

151

'No! I did *not* read your mind! I don't read minds!'

I wish he hadn't said that, she thinks, now he's ruined it and I was beginning to feel so good again, blast the man!

He catches up with her, puts his hand on her arm, slows her and turns her towards him. 'I apologize – that was not a direct and specific reference to you, it's just an expression. People say it all the time and mean nothing by it. Please don't be upset.'

'OK, apology accepted.'

To her surprise he doesn't continue down the hill, he takes a step closer again as if he's trying to see her face. 'What do you do? I mean, what is your job? I don't think it's ever been mentioned.'

'I'm a teacher - science and mathematics.' She smiles as she imagines his expression which she can't see, though they are only a step apart, and though she can't see it, she feels his reaction. 'Believe it or not, I'm actually very much a factual type of person, superstitions and haunted castles don't form part of my belief system. I'll walk under a ladder any day of the week - or volunteer to sleep in a haunted house.'

He chuckles quietly and she smiles, and he says, 'You don't look old enough to be a teacher – how old are you?'

She begins to feel like her normal self, and she is enjoying herself now – sparring with Cosmo might be fun. He was taken by surprise when she said she teaches science, somehow it doesn't fit with his preconceived idea of her, and he has been surprised by what he calls her analytical mind. He has also, like many others, taken her for years younger than she is.

'I'm twenty-eight. How old are *you*?'

Now he smiles; she can't see it, but she knows he's smiling again. 'Serves me right! I thought you were about twenty. I suppose I'll have to start treating you like an adult now. And I'm forty-one, well not quite, my birthday is in a few weeks. I must admit I did wonder about your age during that interview – you were so totally in charge of it, it was a master class in not letting someone manipulate you. And you nearly took over from old Ronald - did you notice how annoyed he was that he couldn't control you?'

'It served him right,' she says vengefully. 'He shouldn't have been so damn devious – he was hoping to trip me up or get me off-balance enough to make a spectacle of myself.'

He chuckles again and she starts down the slope with Cosmo following just behind her, and she thinks how she has misinterpreted that deep chuckle more than once, and how much she actually likes the sound of it.

Getting back into the car and driving away from Okehampton feels like a re-lived experience, as if they have been this close many times before, maybe driving through dark nights in the warm capsule of a car, with no need to talk. Callista sits silent and wonders where this feeling comes from. Is it that being close to Cosmo in the confines of the car is a bit like it was in the lift; they are alone and she feels the whatever-it-is that surrounds him very strongly, like a benevolent shield, stronger than she felt it on the hill ten minutes ago.

And out of the blue, and as surprising to herself as it probably is to Cosmo, Callista turns to look across at him and says quietly, 'Someone left a voodoo doll inside the street door where I live. It was wrapped in brown paper – and there was a card.'

Cosmo glances across at her and she can see how disturbed he is by what she just told him. 'What?! What did you do with it?' He slows, pulls over on the side of the road and turns to look at her.

'I took it to the police and they finger-printed the wrapping and said they will look into it.'

'You felt it harmed you.' He says it as a statement; he knows how to read her feelings. Is it the tone of her voice that enables him to do this or does he actually feel it, like she felt his reactions in the dark at Okehampton?

'Did it involve a threat?' he asks. 'Did some writing come with it?'

She shakes her head, 'No writing, just my name on a white card tied on with string. And there was a large needle through its head, from one temple to the other side, just where I grab hold of my head in that video – and the doll looked quite like me. Dark hair in a ponytail, blue eyes drawn on with marker pen. Someone made it by hand, especially for ... for me. It made me feel strange – I mean, I know they can't actually harm me by doing things like that, but it was an uncomfortable feeling to see it, to know that someone I can't see wants to harm me. It came on the same day that someone gave me this.'

She fishes around in her bag, pulls out her phone and locates the photo of the tweet that Harry had printed out for her, and Cosmo turns the interior light on and reads it out aloud: 'We know who she is, where she is, we have seen the video. She is dangerous and deceitful and must be stopped from fooling the public. She has no real magic. We know what's real, this isn't. If you see her, deal with her, prevent further damage.'

'Do you know who this 'fullmoonmagic' person is?'

She tells him what Harry told her and they sit in silence for a couple of minutes before Cosmo hands the phone back and pulls out on the road. 'I don't like this at all! Some of those who believe in this sort of thing are perfectly OK, but some are probably mentally ill. And that they know where you live – that's not good!'

'We're being careful – that's Becks and I, she's my flat mate. I think I'll get one of those peepholes installed so we can see who's outside our door. And

155

we'll go everywhere together now – well, not tonight obviously, but from now on.'

'Don't go out alone,' he says after a couple of minutes. 'Just don't do it! It's not worth the risk.'

They say little during the rest of the drive to Exeter apart from Callista directing him to her street, but when he stops outside the flat, he gets out of the car and comes around to her side and he looks very serious. 'Callista, do you trust me?'

And to her own surprise she says without hesitation, 'Of course, I trust you!' And then she asks, feeling they have reached a level of understanding she would never have expected a few hours ago, 'And tell me, what do *you* do when you're not debunking supernatural claims made by demented females?'

He takes her by the shoulders and gives her a little shake. 'Aha, sarcasm now? I'm a geologist in one of my other lives. But I'm glad you trust me, that's good – thank you.'

He plants a kiss on her forehead, walks back around the car and drives away.

Callista lets herself into the silent flat and wonders why he said 'in one of my other lives'. It is a strange phrase, and she can't decide if he said it jokingly or if it has a genuine meaning. And if it does, what could it possibly be? Does he have another profession, another interest group like the sceptics or something else again?

Becks' room is dark, and the door is ajar, so she is still out. Callista puts the electric jug on to make a cup of tea and realises that her phone has been on mute since she arrived at the TV studio, and now the screen is full of one-line notifications of emails, texts, Facebook messages. The TV show has generated a huge new wave of interest which she had expected, but this is the reality of it, and it feels like a breach of her privacy to stand in her kitchen seeing the message alerts that have arrived uninvited and gate-crashed her calm. She hesitates and wonders if she should ignore them and look at them tomorrow, but curiosity wins.

Sitting in bed with a cup of tea and two chocolate biscuits beside her, she reads more social media messages and comments than she has ever seen. On the phone screen all the one-liners about social media comments have disappeared now that she has looked at them, but a dozen or more texts messages remain unread. Her mother says, "you handled that brilliantly, very proud of you, will phone tomorrow, you've obviously turned your phone off" and her father says, "it was inevitable, you're flavour of the week, here today gone next week, glad you gave that bastard some of his own back" followed by his standard sign-off, the thumbs-up emoticon.

The last text she looks at is from the same

anonymous phone number as that previous short, but slightly ominous message that referred to Salcombe. This one reads, "Saw you on TV just now, will forward Salcombe video to media soon and make you really famous." There is a smile emoticon at the end of the message, the one that winks, the one she particularly dislikes.

She stares at the message for a long time, reads it again and again and wonders if there is a tinge of maliciousness in it, or if her imagination is making her oversensitive. A threat of further media exposure, yes – but possibly an additional layer of threat. As if the person who sent it is taunting her or wants to punish her for something, though that feeling is probably influenced by all she has been through today.

She picks up the library book Becks has given her with the recommendation that is it un-put-downable and starts reading, but her mind is on other things and not even *Life after Life* can hold her attention. With the book open on her knees, she closes her eyes and leans back against the wall; she can still feel his warm lips on her forehead and his hands on her shoulders, even in retrospect it soothes her anxiety. She recalls his words in the lift, calm words spoken into her hair while he held her, 'I've got you, you're safe, it's OK, I've got you'. She puts the book aside, turns the light off and closes her eyes.

It is a long time before she can sleep. The

anonymous message has left her feeling very uneasy about the possibility that the Salcombe incident will become public knowledge. The media will leap on it like starving hyenas, and it will necessitate new explanations for her Dad about what really happened in Salcombe. Not that she knows what the video shows, if there is a video, or how much of her involvement will be revealed, but she knows he might want a fuller explanation than the brief and evasive description she gave him last year. She lies on her back and thinks of that day last September when her mother came to Exeter for a weekend visit, and they drove down to Salcombe for lunch.

Chapter 18

THE PREVIOUS YEAR

On a sunny September day nearly a year earlier, with a crisp wind from the coast and jackets on the back seat just in case, Callista and her mother set out for a day in Salcombe. The idea was to start early, have an early lunch and, if the weather permitted, walk the track out to Bolt Head, a walk that Liz remembers fondly from her early marriage.

'But isn't it a pity to do it without Dad?' asked Callista when her mother suggested this plan for the day. 'Wouldn't you rather do it with him than with me - and when the orchestra comes back from the tour in a couple of weeks, he'll be so sick of sitting on the bus and lugging his cello around and sitting in rehearsals and sitting on stages - he'll be dying for a good walk somewhere outside a city.'

'We can do that too – no reason why I can't have the pleasure twice. Have you ever done that walk? No? It is lovely, you get great views because you're quite high up on the headland and you can see for miles, and the rock formations! Like fantasy landscapes – you'd love it.'

'We wouldn't get all the way out to the end though, would we? It's looks like quite a distance. Just so we don't end up caught in a sudden rain squall way out there - they said last night there might be showers this afternoon.'

'I think it took about three or four hours, but it's years since we did it last and I can't be sure – I remember we had a picnic lunch out at the very point, it was a wonderful day.'

Arriving in Salcombe, Liz said to Callista, who was driving, 'I had lunch at the Crab Shed when I brought my cousin Fred here a couple of years ago, maybe that would be a good place to stop - the food was good, and I love crabs.'

But Callista had other plans and continued along Cliff Road to South Sands and parked at the back of the beachfront hotel.

'I thought we'd have lunch here. Let's approach it from the other side,' she said and led Liz a few meters back along the road, down beside the boatshed and out onto the sand.

'What a nice little beach this is!' Liz shaded her eyes to look out over the estuary where a few yachts were anchored. 'Bet it's full of families in the summer holidays – perfect for children.' Then she turned and burst out laughing. 'OK, now I know why you wanted me to see it from here! What a surprise – it's practically a clone of the hotel where your father and I stayed on our silver wedding anniversary trip to New England a few years ago. And you remembered it from that photo in the study!'

Callista's plan had been that they would eat on the terrace at the edge of the sandy beach, as she and Harry had done some months ago, on an early spring day. That had not been a happy occasion, due to a barely disguised scene of passive aggression from Harry, which eroded her confidence and enjoyment for the rest of the day and ruined the lunch, but aside from that memory it was a lovely place to enjoy the sun and look out over the estuary.

'No, I'm sorry - not today. It might rain,' said the waiter apologetically, 'so we are only serving coffee outside. We couldn't move you indoors quickly if it starts raining when you're halfway through lunch. If it's still fine when you have finished lunch, you can always move outside for your coffee.'

'Never mind,' said Liz as they lingered over lunch, while the rain swept in from the northeast and they could no longer see the other side of the estuary. 'We'll do the walk another time. There's a shop in Salcombe I would like to visit, so I'll check on my phone and see when they close on a Saturday.'

'Where is Dad right now? They must be about halfway through the tour,' asked Callista as she drove back along Cliff Road towards Salcombe itself. 'Have they done Stuttgart yet? Dad said he was hoping to see an old friend, who lives there. Someone he's not managed to connect with for years.'

'They were there two days ago, and he managed to have lunch with Hans-Christian and his wife. For some reason he was disappointed, but he couldn't quite explain why. He did say Hans-Christian had got very fat, but that can't account for it. But that's happened to me a couple of times when I've met up with someone I knew at school, someone I really liked – they seem to have become a completely different person and all the qualities that made me like them – or admire them – have vanished. Perhaps they never were as interesting as I thought, or life has changed them.'

'Or perhaps you have changed, become more interesting yourself and raised your expectations,' said

Callista and reversed into a parking space that was only just big enough. 'You go ahead, it's very nearly three now - I'll straighten the car up and follow you.'

Liz jogged off along the crowded pavement and disappeared among the pedestrians and Callista followed at a slower pace, looking in the shop windows as she went. The rain was no more than a light drizzle now and occasional glints of sunshine came and went.

She was walking on the outer edge of the pavement to get around a group of people with children and dogs, when a sensation of spoken words appeared in her mind, "there she is, in her pink top - I'll kill the bitch!"

Her brain seemed to short circuit; dizzy and disorientated she nearly stumbled, a sharp stab of pain in her head. She stopped and clutched her head, blinked away the loss of focus – and saw a young woman in a bright pink sweatshirt, just a couple of steps ahead of her, then a car accelerated hard with a screech of tyres behind her. Without thought she flung herself forward, managed to grab the girl's right arm and jerked her violently sideways. They fell hard in a tangle with Callista's arm caught under the girl's body, as the car crashed into the shop window a few steps further along and a shower of broken glass sprayed out. The sound of the impact was like a physical blow, painful and shocking, and Callista put her free arm over her face as a piece of metal landed with a loud bang somewhere very close to her. The quiet after the crash lasted only seconds before shouts and screams erupted and people came running towards them.

She managed to free her arm, got to her feet and stood stunned for a moment staring at the car. Its font was buried deep in the shop, steam was rising from under the bonnet and shards of glass and pieces of metal were strewn everywhere. The airbags had gone off and the driver was trying to open his door which seemed to be stuck; his face was contorted with rage, and he was shouting something she could not hear in the midst of the raised of voices around her.

She turned slowly, dazed and confused, and saw several people on the ground, with blood and glass everywhere. A crowd had formed, and people were kneeling on the pavement among the injured. The girl in the pink sweatshirt was being helped to her feet by two women who led her to one side, her face white and shocked.

With glass crunching under her feet, Callista walked around the rear of the car and continued along the street in the direction she had been going before the crash. All she wanted right now was to get away from the scene and the uproar of people exclaiming and shouting instructions. Traffic had come to a standstill and people were coming out of shops, standing in little clusters staring towards the accident scene. She wove her way between and around them, studying the signs to find the shop her mother had mentioned, still slightly unsteady on her feet until she saw Liz waving a short distance ahead and heaved a sigh of relief.

'My God, that was scary - I nearly had heart failure,' said her mother and led Callista to one side. 'I knew you weren't far behind me, but when I ran out of the shop I couldn't see you behind the car at first, I thought you'd been hit – and look at your arm!'

Callista looked at her left arm, where blood was soaking through the sleeve of her shirt and running down to her wrist, and her mother exclaimed, 'Stop - don't touch it! I can see a piece of glass.'

Holding Callista's arm with one hand she carefully pulled out a slim shard of glass from the slit in the sleeve, and instantly blood flowed faster.

'Press down on it with your fingers, really hard. We need to tie something around it.'

'Here,' said a voice beside Callista and she turned to see a woman holding out a folded blue handkerchief. 'Take this, it's perfectly clean. And give me that piece of glass.' She walked a short distance along and dropped the shard in a bin and returned. 'What can I do?' she said to Liz. 'Is that handkerchief any use? It's not very big.'

'On the diagonal, I think,' said Liz briefly as she folded the handkerchief into a triangle and then into a narrow band. 'Here, this will be long enough.' With the help of the stranger, she folded the shirt sleeve up into a damp and bloodied roll and tied the handkerchief tight over the wound, while Callista stood silent and lost in thought, hardly noticing the people around her.

'Thank you so much!' said Liz to the helpful stranger and led Callista into the shop she had come running out of. 'I wonder if we could have some water and maybe a paper towel.' She pointed at Callista's arm. 'My daughter was cut by flying glass from that accident.'

The shop assistant showed them to a handbasin in the back room. 'Please help yourselves,' she said. 'We haven't got paper towels, but you're welcome to use that box of tissues – and let me know if you need anything else.'

While Liz steadied her arm over the basin and washed the blood away, Callista struggled to make sense of what had happened. Had it really happened the way she remembered? But if it hadn't, how had she known to leap forwards and grab hold of the girl's arm? If I look as confused as I feel, Mum will think I'm in shock, she thought, and then she'll go into full ED nurse mode and sit me down with something sweet, I can just picture it. But I'm not in shock, strangely enough, I know I should be, but I just feel confused. What on earth happened to me back there?

She made an effort to smile and tried to sound normal. 'Thanks Mum – I'll dry my arm. That feels much better – isn't it amazing how much blood came out of that little cut? And thank God it didn't drip all over these jeans, they're nearly brand new.'

'Pity about the shirt, though,' said Liz. 'I've always liked that shirt on you, with the button-down collar - it's the same as the white one, isn't it? But I think it's ruined now.'

Outside they hesitated and stood for a moment looking along the street to where emergency services had arrived, and a large crowd had gathered.

The thought of passing the accident scene was daunting. For some reason Callista would rather not expose herself to people who have already seen her and who might recognize her; a strange instinct, but she felt it strongly.

'Let's go further along and then go back to the car via the back street. I'd rather not try to get past all those people again, it looks chaotic now. We'll just have to reverse half a block if we can and turn down a side street to get out of all this.'

On the way back to Exeter, with her mother insisting on driving, Callista continued to consider if she should mention what had happened or if it was too weird to say out loud. Meanwhile Liz made intermittent comments about careless drivers looking at their phones and how that street should have speed bumps, considering how busy Salcombe always was.

'Mum, listen - something weird happened back there.'

Her mother cast a quizzical glance at her. 'Well, yes – a few seconds earlier or later and you could have been killed. Are you feeling strange, in shock?'

I knew the ED nurse would pop up, thought Callista and smiled to herself. That brisk way of dealing with possible illness, injury or shock – quite bracing, as opposed to lots of sympathy that would probably make me cry.

She started describing what she heard inside her head and her mother slowed, pulled over to the side of the road and turned to face her.

'Would you please start again, darling, from the very beginning, because I'm not sure I understood that first bit. You heard a voice in your head? Like spoken words – and not from someone just behind you? Perhaps you conflated two things, a comment made just beside you and the accident.'

'Oh no! Not something I *heard*, not with my ears– it was *inside* my head. Mum, you've got to believe me! I'm not crazy, I did hear it. It was the weirdest thing – I don't know what it was, but it was as if a voice had spoken inside my head. Not like thoughts, not at all, it was words explicitly voiced – an angry exclamation, but kind of exulting, as if he revelled in some strong feeling, like hate or revenge – definitely a man. And the way he said, "I'll kill the bitch!" – Mum, it was horrible.'

'And then the car came over the pavement and hit the building?'

And Callista realised that she had still not told her the whole story. 'No, Mum – listen, I'll tell you exactly how it was. I heard those words, and they made my head hurt, as if something was bursting inside my skull and my vision dimmed for a moment – and I nearly lost my balance, kind of tripped over my own feet. And then I saw a girl in a bright pink sweatshirt just in front of me, only a couple of steps ahead of me, and at the same time I heard a car accelerating hard behind me and a screech of tyres. It came screaming towards me, so I flung myself forward and I just managed to grab her arm and kind of jerk, I mean the girl in pink - and we both fell. It sounds as if it took several seconds when I say it, but it was all so quick. I don't know how I managed to get a grip on her arm – and I only just did, I got hold of the sleeve of her sweatshirt.'

Suddenly she felt as if she were about to cry; the memory had taken on a life of its own in her mind and made her feel as if she had just avoided being killed for a second time. She sniffled and felt her mother's concerned eyes on her, so she pulled herself together and said, 'I'm not going to cry - but I felt as if I was in real danger again, just for a moment. And the front wheel of that car passed so close, I felt the rush of air and the smell of hot rubber just beside us – and then a terrible crash and glass flying everywhere.'

'You had a very lucky escape, darling! You could have been killed. What did the girl say? Was she all right?'

'I just left,' said Callista baldly. 'I didn't talk to anyone, I just got up and walked away, it was too much just then to try to help. Several people were lying on the ground, maybe four of five - and a dozen people were there in an instant, some were kneeling on the ground in all the glass and debris, helping those who were hurt, and someone lifted the girl to her feet - she seemed to be uninjured. There were lots of people around the car. I couldn't take it - I had to get away, so I walked off and found you.'

Her mother gazed thoughtfully through the windscreen with frown creases between her eyebrows, and Callista sat silent and waited for something: approval, disbelief perhaps, or possibly acceptance. After a couple of minutes that seemed endless, Liz turned her attention back to Callista.

'I don't understand it, and don't worry, that does *not*

mean I don't believe you - it just means that I don't know what to make of it, but I don't doubt your word. If you were the kind of girl who always fantasized and made things up, I might have put it down to the sort of stress that people go through after an accident – sometimes they reconstruct what happened, apply imagined causes, and after a while those details become facts in their mind. We hear and see all kinds of things in ED – injured people describing situations very differently than those who brought them in, who witnessed what happened. Shock can cause all kinds of effects. But you've never been that kind of girl – right from an early age you demanded factual explanations and proof, you took hardly anything on trust.'

She took Callista's hand and held it tight. 'Perhaps this is the kind of nearly unbelievable phenomenon that is best kept to as few people as possible? Can you imagine the interest this would cause – say on social media or in the tabloid press?'

'Awful - it doesn't bear thinking about,' said Callista, relieved now that her story was not being doubted. 'But Mum – I'll probably end up telling Becks, we tell each other everything and it would be good to have someone to talk to about this, apart from you, I mean. I know she looks like she hasn't a thought in her blond head, but you know she's ultra-bright and she's another fact brain - and she can keep a secret.'

'I know, don't forget I've known her since she was

six, and I'm well aware of the brain behind those innocent blue eyes – or seemingly innocent blue eyes.'

She smiled and pulled out on the road behind a campervan, but after a couple of minutes she glanced at Callista. 'Perhaps we shouldn't mention this to your father? You know what he's like – he would press you endlessly for details, theorize about how that voice could be in your head, research it online and never let go of the subject. What do you think? Or would you like to discuss it with him?'

'God no! Let's just tell him about the accident and say I nearly got hit and a piece of glass cut my arm. Nothing about the voice – nothing! He would drive me mad – I do love him, but he can be so obsessive, and I don't want to talk about it all the time. Perhaps I could say I had some kind of premonition that something was about to happen and then he'll be able to say that it was just that I heard the car accelerating that makes me think that, or that I caught a reflection of the car heading for me in a shop window.' She smiles and adds, 'Which will be fine, and it won't be intriguing enough for him to become obsessed with it.'

Her mother returns her smile. 'That's my girl! Just what I was thinking - we'll keep the strangeness of it to ourselves. How about you text Becks now and ask if she would like to come and have dinner with us at my hotel tonight, if she's not doing anything else? And we can tell her about it together and impress on her that she mustn't talk about it. Because I do agree – Becks knowing about it will be good for you, so you can talk to her if you have flashbacks or nightmares. Don't take for granted this is over, darling – it might be with you for some time.'

Chapter 19

THE PRESENT

When Constable Yung calls back in response to Callista's text message at six in the morning a few days later, she says cheerfully. 'Hi Callista, what can I do for you? Has something else happened?'

'Yes and no – nothing bad, but I wondered if you could give me some advice, please. I've had some strange messages, but nothing too bad, no more threats or anything – nothing that needs police action. And no more parcels, thank goodness! But the latest video, the one from the Salcombe accident that appeared on social media late last night – have you seen it?'

'No, I didn't know anything had happened in Salcombe. What happened? Are you hurt?'

Oh no, it's not new, it was in September last year, a

car drove across the pavement and into a shop window, several people were injured. There's a video online now, going viral at the speed of light, and I'm in it.'

'Hang on,' says Mary Yung. 'Give me a moment, I'll get my laptop cranked up and have a look. Is it on Facebook or where did you see it?'

'It's everywhere,' says Callista despondently. 'Absolutely bloody everywhere – Facebook, Instagram, newspaper websites, YouTube, probably being shared a thousand times a minute.'

She can hear Mary tapping away at a keyboard and then she says, 'Right, I've got it, I found it. Just let me watch it - oh my God! What a perfect angle, they got the whole scene - but not so pleasant for you. I imagine you've had enough attention already - and now you'll get heaps more. I saw you on that TV show with the handsome guy - the sceptic, what's his name? Cosmo somebody?'

Callista steels herself to sound reasonable and calm, but she wants to scream. 'Perfect angle, all right! It couldn't be worse if she'd tried. You can see at the beginning that she's filming from diagonally across the street, probably wanting to catch that lovely setting outside the café with the hanging flower baskets? And then I walk into the picture from the right and you can see when that thing happens to me again, just like at Okehampton and ...'

Mary interrupts her. 'Hang on, let me play it again

and have a proper look at the beginning. Oh, wow! Yes, I can see what you mean. I didn't notice the first time – too many people in the frame. Well, *that's* going to add to the media pressure for sure! It's exactly the same as the way you reacted at the castle ruins - you stop suddenly, your hands fly to your temples and you look as if you're stumbling. This time you got moving a lot faster though – or I mean, last September you did, nearly instant action.'

Callista sighs and rubs her forehead hard, as if she could erase all her worries. 'I know, that was because I heard the car coming screaming up from behind, so I knew I only had seconds, or maybe only one second.'

'Great save – brilliant. It seems like your reactions are supercharged when these things happen to you, like you can react faster and run faster than normal – interesting! That bit at the end where you stand there looking around, as if you're making sure everyone is being taken care of, and then you just walk around the back of the car and disappear out of the frame to the left – only one second or so when she got your face straight on. I assume you got some kind of warning that time too?'

'Same thing, yes – I kind of felt that a man said something like 'the pink one' – I can't be sure after all this time and I didn't write it down. And then he said or thought, "I'm going to kill the bitch!" You'll think I'm really stupid, but it has only occurred to me just now that I should have reported it at the time, that it was deliberate, I mean.'

'Now, back up a bit,' says Mary calmly, 'you're not thinking straight. What do you think would have happened if you had reported it? Think about it – nobody would have believed you, not before that very convincing episode at the castle ruins. And it's as clear as daylight from the video that the driver was doing it in purpose, first he's just cruising into the picture slowly and then he suddenly turns and accelerates really fast right over the pavement. I'll check it out in our system and ask a few questions, see what happened afterwards – I'll call you. I've got to get ready now, I have to be out the door in half an hour max. Bye!'

'This is nice,' says Mary later that day and looks around the café two blocks from the school. 'I've never been here before. And they have Bath buns – I haven't had one of those for a while. How did you manage to get away so early?'

'I didn't have a class last thing today, so I got away before any reporters turned up at the school gates. They don't know my timetable, thank God. Lucky for me that you are on that early shift today.'

Mary studies Callista's face for a moment. 'Listen, I can see you're getting stressed – and nobody can blame you, it's been intense from what you told me on the phone. But maybe you should stop running and give them a few prepared sentences to write up. Smile for the camera, say what you said on the TV show – things like "I don't know how it happens" and "it's horrible and I hope it never happens again". Those were such great de-escalating comments, and you could add that bit about how you don't believe in supernatural things - look at how it took the wind out of Ronald's sails, it was the last thing he expected. Tell the reporters stuff like that – give them a little treat, and they might leave you alone, at least for a while. Or say something obviously jokey – make sure they get that it's a joke or an exaggeration. Make them laugh with you, instead of trying to trap you and push microphones in your face.'

Callista sighs. 'I should - that's such good advice because I need to avoid those probing questions about my mental state, or if there's something mis-wired in my brain. It's not that I don't worry about that myself, but it's so hard to talk about it. I don't really like talking to anyone about it. Well. that's not quite true, there's one person I *like* talking to about this whole nightmare.'

Mary lifts her coffee cup and says casually, 'That Cosmo guy, I bet.'

She drinks some of her coffee as if Callista wasn't sitting on the other side of the tiny table, staring in disbelief. She can't believe what she just heard; how could Mary possibly have guessed? Is this middle-aged cop clairvoyant?

'What? What do you mean?' she asks indignantly.

'Hasn't anyone else commented?' Mary laughs quietly at Callista's expression of outrage. 'I thought it was amazing – I watched the repeat of that TV show online just to check, and there's something there right from the start. Kind of like a - well, I don't really know how to describe it, but I sensed it when I watched the show live. That's why I checked it out online as well – in case I had imagined it.' She looks into the distance, as if she is mentally replaying what she saw. 'He watches you, and you do that sideways slanting glance at him more than once and each time one of you looks at the other, something happens – it isn't really visible, so don't ask me how I know it's there at all - but it is.'

'Christ! You are a witch, aren't you? Come on, admit it, somewhere in your ancient Chinese heritage there was someone with magical powers. And would you please explain what you noticed – and I mean in real words, not just vague descriptions. Nobody else has noticed anything that I've heard of.'

Mary Yung is silent for what seems like a full minute, but that's probably not right, thinks Callista and drinks some of her own coffee, but it's a *very* extended pause and I do hope she's going to tell me what she saw – or sensed – because I really want to know.

'Maybe if I were to draw it, it would look like that wifi symbol, you know the one with curved lines fanning out?' Mary draws on the tabletop with her forefinger. 'Or circles on water? I don't know, but to me it's an interesting thing, something I haven't seen before. It fascinated me, so I watched the show again, because I had to see I was right and that it really happened. I'm surprised nobody else has mentioned it.'

Callista hesitates, but only for a moment. This is the first time for a long time, possibly ever, that she has an opportunity to be absolutely frank and open about something intensely personal with someone who has not known her for years, who is not part of her life or went to school with her. It is like confiding in a stranger on a train or a flight; safe in the knowledge that you will probably never meet them again and that you know none of the same people.

'It's like a force field,' she says and looks steadily into Mary's eyes to see her reactions. 'I felt it the moment I set eyes on him - before I had any idea who he was. It radiated out from him and I could physically feel it, like a - maybe a current, a warmth? Or a wave of some kind of energy? Very powerful, anyway - and totally confusing. I went into the make-up room at the TV studio and he was sitting there, and my first reaction, after thinking how good-looking he is, was that he had some kind of strength.' She considers this for a moment and adds, 'Not physical strength, something else.'

'You're a very lucky girl!' says Mary with great

feeling. 'You really are – most people would give an arm or a leg to experience that and I certainly never have! If I read about it in a novel, I'd say it was a load of romantic nonsense, and if someone had suggested I'd be able to pick it up on a TV screen – no way!'

They smile at each other and Callista nearly starts telling Mary about what happened in the lift after the show, but common sense returns and warns her not to leave herself wide open; she knows very little about Mary, after all. The fact that she likes her means little in the context of revealing fascinating details about a current news item; she has probably said too much already. The final straw in this whole dilemma would be to find the story of the lift episode in one of the tabloids. Imagine the headlines on the front page, she thinks and nearly laughs. Endless scope for variations on the theme of 'What went on between the Sceptic and the ESP woman?' or 'Went in enemies and came out hand in hand' - I can't risk that.

'I'm glad you noticed it, though – I thought afterwards it was just my imagination, because it seemed too outlandish to be real. I've thought a lot about that energy field I sensed around him.' She laughs, 'If I believed in ESP and that kind of stuff, I'd say it was like an aura.'

Mary nods at Callista's description of the 'whatever-it-is' that she sensed from Cosmo. 'Exactly what I picked up, but I didn't feel it, of course, I just noticed it.'

She drinks some of her coffee and says mock-accusingly, 'Talking to you is so damn interesting I forgot to drink half my coffee and now it's cold! Never mind – I read up on that crash in Salcombe and I'm surprised you didn't see more about it online at the time. There was one article after he was charged, just a couple of days after the accident - mainly about who he was, a local, not a visitor, and he'd been drinking in a pub for a couple of hours at lunchtime. The girl in pink as they dubbed her, had left him for his best friend a week earlier. He was refused bail on the basis that he was probably a continued threat to her safety, and it emerged that he had taken some so-called substance before he set out to kill her - so he was considered an ongoing risk.'

She makes a face of resigned disapproval. 'The way some guys think their girls are property with no right to change their minds - we see it over and over again. And they use that hateful term 'he stole my girlfriend or wife' as if she was a loaf of bread. Anyway, his case finally came up in February and he got nine years for attempted murder and causing bodily harm to four people, plus the drugs they found in his car, plus the DIC – oh, and he also assaulted the man who levered his door open and got him out after the crash, and he tried to punch a woman who was comforting the girl in pink. Quite a list!'

They part outside and promise to keep in touch, but Mary turns back after a few steps and catches up to Callista. 'Listen, you don't have to worry about me, you've got enough on your mind. When we talk like we did today, that stays between us. I would never share it with anyone. The only exception would be if something happened to you, if something you had told me might have a bearing on it.'

She smiles and walks away and leaves Callista wondering how much of her hesitation, when she nearly talked about the lift, was noticeable. Something must have been, she thinks and walks back to the school, where she has a department meeting to attend. I like Mary, she's very perceptive and she's also very sensible. I wonder if she has children, she would be a great mother. And I might try her advice to talk to those photographers and reporters who stalk me rather than go to all this trouble to avoid them. I wonder if she thinks that something might happen to me. Or was that last comment just what police say routinely when someone tells them a private secret?

· · ·

There are no photographers outside the school when she arrives back for the science department meeting at four, and the feeling of relief lulls her into such a false state of security that the ambush outside the flat takes her completely by surprise. She comes around the corner and before she has time to even put a smile on her face, three reporters cluster in front of her and all talk at once. Their faces are familiar now, but the level of interest has intensified; predictably the release of the Salcombe video has created a surge in media excitement.

'Was the Salcombe warning like the one at Okehampton?' asks the dark-haired woman eagerly. 'Did you feel his thoughts in your mind? Did you know he was aiming for that girl?' Her voice has a carrying quality that makes everything she says sound like an accusation.

An interruption saves Callista from answering. 'Is it true that you have signed an exclusive contract with the Daily Mirror?' asks the blond woman, who Callista now knows is the regional rep for a rival tabloid. 'How much are they paying you?'

The dark woman is holding her phone up. Photo or video? wonders Callista and tries to keep her voice even. 'I haven't entered into any contracts at all.' She smiles with some effort. 'I haven't even replied to those who have sent offers - I'm simply not interested.' She tries to look lighthearted. 'It's not that I don't appreciate you guys stalking me, you understand, it's just that I have nothing to say.'

Now the blond woman has her phone aimed at her too, probably video, thinks Callista, so I'd better get this right and not say anything silly and lose my advantage.

'But what if someone offers a big amount? Huge money?' asks the bearded man who hardly ever actually asks anything. 'Surely you would accept it – what if they offered you ten thousand quid? Nobody would blame you for taking it.'

On an impulse Callista decides that maybe Mary is right, interaction will give the impression of being friendly, and if she can make them think there's no point in chasing her, all the better.

'Are you offering *that* much?' She looks straight at him and grins. 'I might even go on a date with you if there was that much on the table.'

The blond woman laughs. 'You wouldn't have him for a bit less. Like half?'

Callista pretends to study the man's face more closely, then she shakes her head, 'No, sorry – no offence intended, but no.'

She can feel the atmosphere changing, like a change in air pressure. They are relaxing, enjoying the repartee and she hopes both those phones are recording video.

The dark woman raises her voice. 'But if you got one of those warnings that you get – say it was about this guy here, and he was about to be attacked, you *would* save him, right?'

'I think so,' says Callista and pretends to consider this. 'Yes, I probably would, unless I was in a real hurry.'

Now they are laughing, and she takes the opportunity to extricate herself. 'Sorry guys, but I really have to go inside now. If my mum sees me talking to strangers I'll be grounded for a week.'

They part and let her walk the last few yards to the door without further questions. So that's it, she thinks, as she climbs the stairs feeling worn out. Make friends with the press, disarm them with nonsense and so long as they get something to quote, however irrelevant, they might leave me alone.

Chapter 20

On the way to school a couple of days later, Becks says, 'I've just remembered that couple who came early that morning. I completely forgot about them – they never sent an email after all.'

'They did – but they sent it to me.' Callista gets her phone out of her bag. 'I don't know how they got hold of my email address, but they sent it the next day and I forgot to tell you. They want me to ... hang on, I'll read it out to you, it's so sad.'

She scrolls through her emails and sighs. 'I get so many now – everyone who ever had my address wants to ask me about one thing or another. Oh, here it is – they want to know if I can, and this is their words, "help us find our son who disappeared thirty-four years ago aged three from a beach in Dorset. The police never found any leads and we have never known what became of him. We still have some of his toys and clothes, so we can give you something that belonged to him to help you sense where he is or what happened to him." Isn't it sad that this horrid fame of mine made these poor parents think that I'd be able to help them? It makes me feel like a fraud. I wrote them a long reply and said I really can't, and they would be better to search out a reputable medium.'

'Oh, God! That's heartbreaking – and I was so short with them when I opened the door that morning. I feel so guilty now. But a medium? Really?'

'I had to give them something, Becks! I couldn't just say no, and what else could I suggest? Not that I believe in mediums, but it was the only thing I could think of.'

On the way to the staff cloakroom, the Head once again catches up with them. 'I wonder if you could say something at tomorrow's Weekly Assembly?' he asks Callista with a look of slight embarrassment. 'There are so many rumours among both students and staff, but I think you could put their minds at rest, if you address them yourself.'

'What does that mean? Put their minds at rest? What have you heard?'

He clears his throat and sounds uncomfortable, avoids looking her in the eye. 'It seems that some people think, or perhaps worry is a better word, that you can read their minds. Apparently, you said something to a boy in your Year 11 science class last week that made him think you read his mind – something about magnesium? And it has spread like wildfire among the students. I've had a few calls from parents too, and I expect more will come. People latch on to anything like this – they love the mysterious quality of it.'

Callista thinks for a moment and realises that the only way to shut down this silly rumour is to tackle it head-on. 'OK, I know what that thing about magnesium was,' she says, reluctantly. 'I could tell you now, but if you try to explain it to parents, they probably won't believe you, so I perhaps I had better do it myself.'

'Good! I am very grateful,' says the Head with relief in his voice at not having met any opposition this time. 'And anything else you can think of that might benefit from being ... shall we call it "de-escalated"? Anything you can think of. I'll call you up at the end of Assembly.'

He turns and walks back towards his office and Becks stares at Callista with a crease between her eyebrows. 'Now what have you been up to? This is unbelievable – one thing after another. We might have been right a while ago when we said you would have to move or change your name. What happened in class?'

'I don't want to talk about it here where people will

come past and hear us, but it's just nonsense - I'll tell you on the way home. And isn't it funny that the Head always just *happens* to spot you in a hallway whenever he wants to talk to you? I bet he lies in wait behind some strategic corner in the mornings, so he can come up behind you and pretend it's just chance that he saw you,' says Callista. 'Let's get a move on, Becks, the bell will go any minute!'

But on the drive home Becks forgets to ask and Callista decides not to remind her, and when they get upstairs, they are distracted by a brown parcel beside their door. It is a bigger one this time, rectangular and solid looking, wrapped in brown paper and once again tied neatly with string.

'Don't touch it!' Becks drops her book bag on the floor and takes hold of Callista's hand and pulls her back. She gets her phone out and calls the police while Callista stares at the package and listens to Becks talking, without taking in a single word.

'They'll send a car.' Becks unlocks the door. 'They said to leave it where it is, someone will be here in fifteen minutes. Come on, don't stand there – come in and put your gear down. We'll leave the door open a crack so we can hear them coming up the stairs.'

They put their things away in silence, unable to think of anything to say. Normal conversation seems impossible and when they hear footsteps on the stairs, Becks says quickly, 'Stay here, I'll see who it is.'

'Hi there,' says Mary Yung when she sees Callista appear behind Becks. 'This is Malcolm, he's my partner today. So, this is the parcel – looks as if it was wrapped by an expert, very tidy. Have you got a pair of sharp scissors?'

'What!? Are you going to open it before you fingerprint it?' asks Becks. 'I kind of expected the bomb squad or something.'

'We'll have a peep without doing anything drastic,' says Mary calmly and pulls on vinyl gloves. 'Come on, Malcolm, get your gloves on. Scissors?' she adds and looks at Becks, who obediently fetches the kitchen scissors.

Mary directs Malcolm to hold the box steady on the edge of the top step, just touching it with his gloved fingertips while she goes down three steps and crouches with the scissors in her hand.

'I'll cut the string on the side here and just open the end flaps and see what I can see.' She peers into the parcel and then she looks up at Callista, who stands with Becks in the doorway, and smiles. 'Ah, yes – it's a giant box of Cadbury Milk chocolates, still with the cellophane wrapping around the box – looks OK.' She cuts through the string in three more places and pulls the folds of paper apart.

'Here's a card – do you want me to read it, or do you want to do it yourself?'

She holds up a large card with a picture of kittens in a basket and Callista starts to laugh. 'Oh, my God! I bet I know who put this here.'

She reaches for the card and nods. 'Yep! It's from old Mrs. Thurston, Becks. It says, "I was so sorry to hear about all the trouble you are having, so I thought some chocolates might help." How funny, I knew the moment I saw the card that it would be from her.'

She turns to the two police officers still crouching on the stairs. 'She was our landlady when we first came to Exeter – we had a bedsit in her house, she was a lovely landlady. Bring the parcel inside, Mary – we'll open the box, and all have some chocolates.'

The headmaster says, 'Miss Bannister, would you like to come forward, please?' at the weekly assembly the next morning, and Callista walks to the front and takes the microphone. She feels the attention from six hundred and thirty-eight students like a wave of pressure flowing towards her and curling around her, and the intensity of their focus is unlike anything she has felt before. This must be what it is like to be a star on a stage with the masses waiting to hear what you are going to say, she thinks and takes a deep breath to steady her inner self.

'I've promised the headmaster to talk to you about what happened at Salcombe and Okehampton,' she says and lets her eyes slowly scan the faces of her audience. 'It's been described as a trick, or a fraud, or perhaps magic, or extra-sensory perception, which simply means knowing what's in another person's mind.'

She smiles and moves her head slowly from side to side, indicating surprised amazement. 'But I don't know what it was – I can't explain it any more than anyone else can. All I can do is tell you how it happened and what it has meant for me, for my life. I have no idea what caused it, certainly not anything I did or wished for. It just arrived like a bolt of lightning from a blue sky – unexpected and terrifying.'

She tries to sound relaxed. 'But before I start on that, I want to talk a bit about this rumour that I can read people's minds. I know where it came from and it was simply that strange kind of thing that happens now and then when you're thinking something and somebody else says exactly that, or something that relates to it - just a chance coincidence. It happened in a class last week when a student was thinking about magnesium – God knows why – and I happened to say the word a second later. It seemed spooky, but it was just that kind of coincidence. And I'm very pleased that I can't read your minds. I'm sure I'd be shocked and horrified if I knew what you lot think of in class - and then I'd be obliged to tell your parents and it would become very complicated and maybe embarrassing. So, your secrets are safe from me.'

She smiles and looks around the hall again and tries to make them all feel included. 'But at Salcombe last year, something very odd happened to me. I had a sudden idea spring into my head that something terrible was going to happen and then I heard a car accelerating very fast from behind me, coming towards me. And apparently, I leapt forward and grabbed the arm of girl just in front of me, a girl who would have been hit by that car if I hadn't pulled her to one side – that's what we've seen on the video someone posted on social media, but I can't actually remember doing that in any detail. The girl and I fell to one side, and there was an almighty crash when the car hit the shop window - I was as shocked and surprised as everyone else.'

I'm not telling them the full story, she thinks, not after what I said on TV, I've got to keep it straight and leave the details out, the words I heard in my head and how I knew it was that particular girl he was aiming at. If I contradict myself, nobody will ever believe me again.

She sweeps her eyes across the hall once again, tries to make them feel that she is talking to them individually on a personal basis.

'And then a year later at Okehampton it happened again, but in a different way. I felt very strongly and very precisely that the man, who had stopped some ten metres in front of me on the hill by the old ruins, was armed and intent on hurting or killing people. I tried to convince others to help me stop him, but they thought that I was crazy, of course, which isn't surprising. So, I did what the urgent feeling inside me told me to do, I tried to stop him by myself.'

You could hear a pin drop, she thinks, this hall has never been so totally silent before, it's very strange, as if they are holding their collective breath.

'So, that's what caused this uproar - two events that involve me and neither of which I can explain – and it has caused me a lot of grief, but I can't do anything about it, I have no answers. I have been sent threatening letters and people have posted horrible things about me on social media. I have been hounded by reporters and photographers, and someone left a parcel at my flat with a voodoo doll that looks very like me, that somebody made very carefully with the aim of hurting me – the doll had a pin stuck through its head. But some people have been lovely, concerned about how this has made me feel, and how hard it is to cope with. I've been given boxes of chocolates and received kindness from strangers, and that has made me able to continue with life in an ordinary kind of way, even on the days when I would rather stay in bed and pretend the rest of the world doesn't exist. Thank you all for listening – and remember, however intriguing and interesting this seems to others, to me it is something frightening that I don't understand, and I can only hope it never happens again.'

'That was perfect,' says Becks when the students have left the hall and half the teaching staff have hugged Callista. 'So quietly powerful and such a good way of telling them how hard this is for you. Well done!'

'Bye!' calls Becks when she leaves the flat straight after dinner that night to go for a walk with Dudley. 'Don't open the door to anyone you don't know, please – and don't eat all those chocolates.'

Callista stays where she is on the living room sofa with her book open on her knees, but she is not reading, she is too troubled by her own thoughts to concentrate. Somehow, she was sure that she would hear from Cosmo, she felt they had established a bond, but he seems to have vanished over the horizon, as if the strangely intimate time in the lift and then again on the Okehampton hill never happened. Perhaps it didn't mean anything to him, other than just an interesting encounter, she thinks, a passing moment in his life and now he has moved on. The silence from him makes her feel vulnerable, as if her perception that they shared something significant, that she meant something to him, is just a trick of her imagination.

When there is a noise on the stairs, she sits very still and listens as the footsteps stop, the doorbell rings and someone runs downstairs. The door to the street slams shut and she waits a few minutes, wonders if it is a trick to make her open the door incautiously and then she laughs at herself and goes to see if there is anything outside. Possibly another doll, she thinks, or something even less pleasant, but I can't shy away from reality, I'll just go and look, or I'll sit here worrying about it until Becks comes in.

Leaning against the door frame is a large bouquet of flowers wrapped in cellophane; the biggest and most expensive bunch of flowers she has ever received. Standing at the kitchen bench, trying to think what they have that is tall enough to put them in, she delays opening the card. Don't be an idiot, she tells herself, just open the damned thing – you're only hopeful because you just thought of Cosmo, get a grip!

It is from the staff at school, a large card with lots of signatures and little drawings – a show of support that nearly makes her cry.

Back on the sofa with the flowers leaning into the corner by the window to make them a bit more stable in the vase that is nowhere near tall enough, she hears her phone give a message alert. 'Watch YouTube video, title Callista's talk, very good! Love Dad.' And two seconds later another message, this time from Harry: 'Check out the video, just posted link on Twitter – brilliant!'

Her entire talk at the Assembly has been filmed by a student and is now being widely shared, and she sits for a long time thinking of how social media can be such a curse and a blessing at the same time. She pins her hopes on time calming things down and that the Assembly video will damp down some of the inflated rumours that have spread about her.

But will I ever have a truly normal life again now that my name is a byword? Perhaps years from now I'll see that glint of recognition in someone's eyes when I'm introduced. Perhaps that half joking conversation Becks and I had about me changing my name is the answer, after the immediate interest has died down?

'Good morning, this is sergeant Purdy,' says a voice with a north country accent, when Callista answers her phone early the next morning. She has just come out of the shower and tries to dry her hair off with one hand while she holds the phone with the other and drops of cold water from the ends of her hair trickle down her back and make her shiver.

'We have some good news for you, we've been in touch with Vanessa Saunders also known as "fullmoonmagic" - and after a conversation with a senior police officer and a verbal warning, she has agreed to take down all social media posts that could be seen as threatening your safety. It will be done by midday today and we are going to follow up to see that it's done. She doesn't appear to have had anything to do with the voodoo doll and said – I'll read out what's on my screen "voodoo dolls are just a superstition and have nothing to do with real magic". I thought you might like that rather odd comment.'

'Well, that's one down,' says Callista and continues to dab at her wet hair with the towel. 'What kind of warning did she get? Just out of interest – was it just saying, "Don't do this again" or something specific?'

'I get the impression it was made in general terms, but it says in the notes that the officer referred to the potential charge of inciting violence against a person, so pretty serious stuff.'

'Is she local?'

'No, she lives in a village outside Cardiff.'

'Miss Bannister - I've got something for you!' calls Miss Watson from her window, when Callista and Becks come around the corner of the main building. 'I'll give it to you now instead of putting it in your pigeonhole - it came by courier just before I left yesterday afternoon.'

She leans out the window, drops a small courier bag into Callista's hands and retreats inside. They continue in through the staff entrance and Becks looks at the way Callista holds the bag away from her body with one hand and says suspiciously, 'It's not a bomb, is it? Has someone threatened to blow you up? No, really – I mean it. After all the other stuff that's been going on – nothing feels very safe any longer. I think we should cut it open with scissors – right here and very carefully and just peek inside.'

Callista stops and turns her hand so she can see the back of the bag. 'No sender. Maybe we should – not that I think it is a bomb, but it could be something smelly or offensive. Who knows what this damn fame will conjure up next from the lunatic fringe? Could be anything.'

She puts the bag on the tiled floor of the staff cloakroom and Becks runs off to find a pair of scissors. When she returns Callista still stands there looking at it with a strange expression on her face.

'What?' says Becks. 'What's wrong?'

'I don't know. So many things seem weird to me now, like the world has shifted on its axis - like what I thought was up, is now sideways. I can't explain it, and it's possible I'm just overly alert to ... everything, but this bag gives me the creeps. Could you please open it for me?'

Becks gets down on her knees and when a pair of

boots appear beside her, she says without looking up. 'Hi Arnold, Callista is worried about this anonymous bag – what do you think?'

'I'm not surprised,' says the man wearing the boots, puts his motorbike helmet on the floor and kneels beside Becks. 'You're getting famous Callista. Do you want a hand, Becks?' He turns and squints up at Callista. 'You're not really worried it's a bomb, are you?'

'No, I think it's probably just something I'd rather not see.'

Becks and Arnold look at each other, then Becks holds the bag steady and Arnold cuts it open and peers inside. 'A white envelope,' he announces and pulls it out, runs it between his fingers first one way and then the other. 'Seems to contain nothing but paper – nothing thick.'

He hands it to Callista, and she slowly inserts her forefinger at the upper corner and rips the envelope open. There is a single sheet of paper inside, a ruled page from a notepad with a note written with a blunt pencil. The others stand silent beside her, Becks with the empty courier bag in her hand, and the cloakroom is totally silent while Callista reads the letter, then she folds it in half again.

'Just anonymous nonsense - but no threats. Thank God!' and smiles and hopes she looks completely relaxed. Becks, who is usually hard to deceive, says,

'Throw it away! You don't want to keep anything anonymous - the very word is nasty.'

Arnold looks more searchingly at her. Maybe he picked something up while I scanned those few lines, she thinks, he's a very quiet chap, perhaps he's observant too. She smiles at him and says, 'I hope you're not disappointed – you walked in on a what seemed like a real-life drama, and it turns out to be nothing. I'll do better next time!'

'No problem – always glad to help,' says Arnold, hangs up his helmet and jacket and heads for the staff room after a lingering look at Becks.

'Another one captivated?' Callista raises her eyebrows at Becks. 'I didn't realise.'

'Just a crush, nothing serious – he's nearly over it,' says Becks callously, as she walks over to the rubbish bin in the corner and drops the courier bag in it. 'He thought he was in love with me, but it's mostly worn off now.'

'Someone should do a research study of whatever it is that you emit – some mega-potent pheromone that could probably be isolated and bottled and sold for a fortune. I wonder what they'd call it - 'Come Hither' or maybe 'Sex in a bottle'?'

'Don't be silly!' says Becks. 'I need to pee, see you later.'

As soon as she has disappeared, Callista picks the courier bag out of the rubbish bin and tucks it into her bag. She unfolds the sheet of paper and reads it again.

In case you do not know about where you come from and they might not have told you but you are probably mad like your bioligogical biological father, he believes in crazy things ask your mum. I don't believe all that nonsense you say happened I see in the paper that he is Sir Anthony now you do look very like him.

Dismal punctuation, but mostly spelled right, she thinks, as she refolds the paper and puts it in her bag. I'm not going tell anyone about this until I've asked Mum what it might mean. Could it be true? Is Dad not my biological father? I don't understand why someone would send this out of the blue and for no reason, just make it up – surely, it must mean something, but I can't imagine my parents not telling me, if this is really true. They're not the sort of people who hide things – or maybe I was adopted, and I'm not their child at all. I don't think anything in this whole saga of strangeness has surprised me as much as this letter, it's like being hit over the head from behind. I feel quite weird now, not only are the natural laws not what I have always believed, but maybe I am not what I've taken for granted that I am either. And Sir Anthony – how many of those are there? Probably dozens. If Becks asks, I'll say I've thrown it away. I'll do nothing about this until I've had time to digest it. I suppose I should be grateful it wasn't something toxic or threatening – the possibility of having a stranger for a father might come to seem quite manageable compared to the rest.

Chapter 21

That night Callista is in the kitchen making a chicken, camembert and spinach pie, when Becks calls out from the living room where she is watching the TV news. 'Come quick! It's about you!'

Callista arrives just in time to hear '... by Cosmo St Clair, well-known spokesman for Sceptics in Science.'

'I missed it! What did he say?'

'He wasn't on, they just quoted what he said. I suppose they called him - they're always asking him for comments when something not very rational is being discussed. They played that video from Salcombe first – my God, you were so quick, darling. Unbelievable, I can't stop watching it online – I mean, I've always known you're athletic in a kind of casual non-competitive way, but that leap forward when you grabbed her arm and pulled her to the side - unreal!

He would have got her for sure if you hadn't done that.'

'But what did he say?'

'Oh, he just said the usual things - that there has never been the slightest concrete evidence to prove that ESP works the way it is popularly believed to. And something about – no, I can't remember that bit, must have been when I was shouting to you.'

'No, it wasn't! Remember you're talking to the only person in the world who isn't deceived by those blue eyes. Come on, Becks! What did he say?'

'Just something about how ESP gets a lot of attention, like other mystical beliefs and that people are very gullible, they like unexplained mystical things.' She stops talking and looks blandly at Callista who is standing in the kitchen doorway with a knife in her hand.

'Becks!' she says ominously and brandishes the knife. 'What *else* did he say?'

'Oh, all right then – he said those who claim to experience it often exaggerate, encouraged by the media attention they always get, they kind of add detail.'

'Blast the man! How dare he?' Callista turns her back before Becks can see how upset she is. What she just heard feels like a stab in the back, a real betrayal of her trust. How could he, she thinks, and blinks hard, what a shitty thing to do. He makes me trust him and asks if I do - and I, idiot that I am, I say that yes, I do trust him, of course I do – and then he goes public with a dismissive statement like that.

She cannot quite understand why she feels so bereft, but it is as if something that anchored her safely in this new existence of press harassment and innuendo, some kind of safety barrier, has suddenly proved to be an illusion. She is thankful now that she never told Becks about Cosmo driving her home from Plymouth and their stop at Okehampton. Somehow the strangely intimate feel of the whole Cosmo encounter seemed so private and precious, like something that might evaporate into thin air if she talked about it. It is one of the very few times since they were six years old that she has not told Becks about a significant event.

She puts pastry over the top of the pie, turns the dish and presses the edge down so hard it nearly overturns. Closing the oven door around it, she sets the timer, goes to her room and shuts the door. She cannot stop thinking about the quote from Cosmo on the news and lies on her bed remembering her reaction to him at various times, tries to find evidence for her belief that he would not let her down, that he held her in some sort of affection and respect.

But what have I based that belief on? she thinks,

why have I felt it so strongly from the first time I saw him in the TV studio, when I felt that indefinable pull towards him, though all we said was 'hi'. And then during the interview, not only did I think that he was kind of protecting me a couple of times from some of that creep's questions, but I felt that other sensation again, that aura that surrounds him and I thought it was aimed at me – just at me, not something others would feel. And if it was not, then why was he so caring and comforting in the lift and sat holding me while I slept. And when he dropped me off, he asked me if I trusted him. I'm a stupid fool, those things meant nothing, I just wishfully imagined they did, because I feel so attracted to him. I need to stop reading things into what people say and do without any direct evidence. I'm supposed to be a fact person, for God's sake.

'Are you at work? I need to talk to you,' Callista texts her mother, when Becks leaves straight after dinner to go to the movies. Talking to Liz about the letter has become an urgent issue in her mind and she feels a need to do it without the least possibility of being overheard or having her reaction after the conversation with her mother observed by anyone, not even Becks, whatever that reaction will turn out to be.

The most important thing is to just hear the truth,

and she no longer feels concerned about the effect it might have on her relationship with her parents, not even her father. What worries her is that she might be about to find out that her biological father is someone she would rather not know about. And what did that comment in the letter mean about him being mad? Mad as in 'insane'? Or has he done something 'mad' – perhaps a crime? Maybe he murdered someone. She has wanted to talk to her mother ever since she heard what Cosmo said on TV, but she knew she couldn't call her and not mention the letter. I'm not nervous, she thinks, I just need to know – and then I'll feel better about everything.

'Will call in 20 mins, just watching end of film,' texts Liz and Callista gets the anonymous letter out of her bag and puts it on the table beside her phone. She doesn't try to deceive herself into thinking that this is not going to be a potentially emotional conversation, and busies herself with tidying up in the kitchen, unable to sit still.

'Right!' says her mother half an hour later. 'How is it going with those reporters – we saw you on TV as I said in a text the other day, with that cluster of them waiting to waylay you outside the flat. What a splendid performance - and clearly the perfect tone to take, make then laugh, give them something to quote and they'll go away, at least for a couple of days.'

'It might not last, Mum. It has died down just a bit,

but I don't know how long it will last. You see, I got an anonymous letter, sent to the school by courier, and if the person who wrote it sends a copy to the press too, then I'm in for it – any personal detail about me will add to my so-called fame. Those reporters will pitch a tent on the doorstep and never leave.'

'Was it a threatening letter?' Liz sounds concerned. 'Did you hand it over to the police?'

'I'll read it out to you, and I can send a photo of it, if you would like to see it.'

She reads the message, trying to keep her voice neutral and when she has finished there is silence for a long moment before Liz says, 'Damn it! I *knew* we should have told you, but your father was totally against it, we nearly had a fight over it.'

'Is it true! Is Dad not my father? And who is this Sir Anthony? For God's sake, Mum, why didn't you tell me? I can't believe you just left me to find out from a stranger!'

She hears herself sounding outraged and thinks how odd it is, that she didn't feel outraged before, just surprised and curious. As if talking about it has just made the potential consequences of the letter more threatening and important than they were before she voiced the question.

'Darling, listen to me - I'll tell you the whole story. Your father is at a rehearsal, they are starting this year's tour next week and they have rehearsals every second day. They've included a new piece, very modern and it's causing some difficulties, the violins are finding it particularly challenging. Have you got a glass of wine in your hand?'

'No, Mum! I do not have a glass of wine in my hand! Am I going to need it?'

'You might,' says her mother coolly. 'I'm not sure if you will or not, but a glass of wine is always helpful, don't you think? I have one right beside me.'

Callista can picture her mother in her customary armchair in the living room with her feet tucked sideways under her, the standard lamp behind her the only light in the room and a glass on the round table beside her chair. Somehow the familiar image only serves to make her more nervous, as if what she is about to hear might change her world forever, but she goes to the kitchen and pours herself a glass from the bottle of red that sits open on the bench.

'This is how it was,' says Liz. 'I met your dad and we fell head over heels in love at twenty – I was a nursing student, and he was at the school of music. We got married as soon as we were both qualified and after four years, I was twenty-six then, we discovered that he was sterile, totally sterile. He had mumps with double orchitis when he was pre-pubertal, but he had never known that it might have made him sterile - and it is quite rare that boys in that situation become completely sterile, but he was. So, we had two choices –

adoption or sperm donation. The process for fertility treatments wasn't as streamlined and easy then as it is today and a lot of people simply solved the problem themselves, using sperm from a donor they knew, or a relative.'

Callista listens and thinks that this is the fringe benefit of having a mother who is a nurse; there is no attempt to be other than factual or use the right terminology, but she must check up on a orchitis, a word she has never heard before. And Liz hasn't mentioned how they did it, or who donated the sperm. If it was not done in a hospital setting, they must have used the turkey baster method. She has read about this, but never thought it would apply to her. Was she a turkey baster baby?

'Any questions?' asks her mother. 'Apart from the obvious one about why we didn't tell you, but I'll explain that and try to make you understand.'

'Of course, I have questions!' says Callista crossly. 'To start with – who is this Sir Anthony person? And why him?'

'He is, or was, a reasonably famous conductor and he lectured at the music school in those days. Lovely man, you look just like him, tall and slender with black hair and the most marvellous dark blue eyes. All the female music students were infatuated with him and some of the men too. Your Dad really admired him, and they've performed together since, too.'

'Did you know him? Even if you weren't a music student. And how did you get him to agree to it?'

'Your Dad did that – we discussed it, talked about who we knew who'd have good genetic material and maybe, if possible, someone who was musically gifted. Your Dad really wanted that, and he simply asked Anthony – he didn't have his knighthood then, of course – and he said yes, he'd be honoured.'

Callista sits mesmerized, trying to picture her parents as they were then, as she has seen them in photographs, young and happy with her as a newborn. She drinks some of her wine and says, 'And why didn't you tell me? Why let me discover it like this, by chance and from a stranger – and I don't even know who wrote that letter.'

Liz sighs. 'I wanted to tell you, darling. When you were four or five I suggested we bring it up in some way that would make sense to you and then we'd be able to introduce the subject now and then in a casual way until you were older and had the full picture, but your Dad was so against it! It made him so upset, that I gave in. I think he worried that you would want to search out your biological father and that you might bond with him, and it would change the family dynamics. I'm sorry, darling! I should have told you anyway.'

'Were you infatuated with him, like all those students of his were? With Anthony?'

'Oh no, not at all, but it was easy - he was a

charming and good-looking forty-something man with great sex appeal - and he knew how to please.'

Callista nearly chokes on her mouthful of wine, she can't believe her ears. Is Liz saying she went to bed with Anthony to conceive?

'Mum! Did you sleep with him? Is that what you're saying?'

'I did – it was by far the most reliable method, far more likely to succeed than using a baster. We only did it a few times and then I was pregnant. Why – are you shocked? I didn't think anyone of your generation would be shocked at that! Heavens, Callista – even if you haven't done it yourself, you must have friends who do it - buddy sex, friends with benefits, call it what you will. It was just sex, Callista, not love, not betrayal!'

'And Dad was OK with this? It didn't freak him out and make him feel left out or jealous?'

'Oh no, maybe it's because he's an oddball and he doesn't react like most other people do, but he accepted that this was the best way of doing it - and he was so excited about us being able to have child. He probably sat down and listened to a symphony or practiced something while I was at Anthony's place. I would come home, and we'd have a cup of tea and talk and that was it. And he was besotted with you from the moment he saw you, and so proud of you.'

'Despite the fact that I don't seem to have a musical bone in my body?'

Her mother laughs. 'He's never mentioned it after that time when you were six or seven and your piano teacher said she would prefer not to teach you because she thought you might be tone deaf, you couldn't follow a tune at all. We just laughed about it and let you stop. Genetics isn't an exact science. And anyway, I'm like that too, I never hum or sing when your Dad can hear me – he says it gives him a physical pain.'

'And what about Anthony? Is he alive? Has he got other children – what if I fall in love with an unknown half-brother and have to part from him, devastated and heartbroken? Has he ever seen me? And what's his name, his full name?'

Her mother laughs again, relieved to hear Callista's voice change to her usual half serious, half mocking tone.

'His name is Anthony Williams and he retired from conducting a couple of years ago. He lives somewhere in Dorset now, in a cottage he had for holidays. He never married and he has no other children that I know of. Well, I'm pretty sure actually – he said once to your Dad, years after you were born, probably about the time you went to university - that he was glad he had done it, so there was one copy of his DNA in the world. Oh, and he said that he had left documentation with his legal people saying that you're his biological daughter.'

She is silent for a moment and before Callista gets

around to the next question, her mother adds. 'Funny, I never thought of that before, never entered my head! But now that I've said it out loud, it makes me wonder. Why would he leave that information with his lawyers? I bet he's made a will in your favour or at least left you something. Mind you, he's not dead yet, he's only about seventy-six I think, you might have to wait another twenty years to find out!'

While Callista has a slight mental hiccup over this surprisingly mercenary statement, or possibly just pragmatic, Liz adds exactly the thing Callista has been thinking about. 'Do you want to meet him?'

'I don't know. I'll need to think about it, but I don't think so. Why does that letter say he's mad? Is he mentally ill or something?'

'I think it's because he has some quite unusual interests, like numerology and a couple of other things. And he's always been quite a one for writing letters to the editor and having opinions on every subject under the sun, these days he probably blogs. I know he believes in reincarnation, I read it somewhere a few years ago, he said in an interview that he hoped to be reincarnated as an elephant, he was quite serious. And I'm sure he's following everything that's happened to you with great interest, just his cup of tea, something like this that can't be explained. Not that I know that, but he knows your name, of course, and you look just like him – and only someone who's been in a coma could be unaware of your fame now.'

'And you're not in touch with him?'

'No, I haven't seen him since I knew for sure I was pregnant. Your Dad has played under him a few times, and when I asked him if they spoke about you, he said 'of course not, it would be completely out of context' – he never ceases to amuse me, your Dad. I imagine that time Anthony made the comment about his DNA was the only time they ever mentioned it – they weren't close friends of anything, different generations really, more than twenty years apart in age.'

When she says goodbye to her mother, Callista turns on her laptop and searches the internet for "Anthony Williams, conductor". Photos appear instantly, followed by articles, reviews and details about his life and career. He is variously mentioned as a mentor of talented students, a keen supporter of the Historic Places Trust and many other worthy things. His conducting career seems to have made him mid-range famous and the knighthood was awarded after many years of organizing fundraising concerts for the Historic Places Trust. But the photos are an eye-opener; Callista can see the strong likeness in those from thirty years ago. She squints at them and tries to picture what he would look like as a female and decides they would be very alike.

Could have been a lot worse, she thinks, and curls up in the corner of the sofa with another glass of wine. He could have turned out to be one of those men, who are revealed to be child molesters later in life or who have committed some dreadful crime. Having a genetic father who is very handsome, talented and generous isn't bad. But Dad will always be my Dad, and however much Mum and I laugh at him at times, that's not going to change.

She sends a text message to Liz and says: All good here, nothing's changed, still love my oddball dad. No particular wish to meet Sir A.

And then she sends one to her Dad too and tells him she loves him and wouldn't swap him for anything in the whole world. She has no idea if Liz is going to tell him about the anonymous letter, but it doesn't matter now; she feels as if she is back on an even keel. Maybe I'm a bit odd too? Does this seem too easy? Perhaps I inherited my mother's pragmatic gene as well as her tone deafness.

When Becks comes back after the movie, she finds Callista still there with the half empty glass in front of her and says in surprise, 'You *never* drink on you own – are you OK? Is the press ganging up on you again – ha-ha, see what I did there? But seriously, are you all right?'

'I'm fine, thanks. Have a glass - there's some left in that bottle on the bench. And I feel a lot better now that I might have found the right way of dealing with the press.'

They sit talking until midnight and Callista goes to bed feeling, if not normal, at least better than she has since she first read the letter on Monday.

Chapter 22

When her phone pings with a text alert at six in the morning a few days later she nearly buries it under her pillow and goes back to sleep, but curiosity about who is sending a message so early makes her sit up and pick the phone up. The one-liner on the screen shows it is from someone whose phone number she doesn't have in her Contacts, starting with the sentence: *Are you OK? I see you ...*

She checks the rest of the message, but there are only a few more words and the entire message reads, *Are you OK? I see you developed magic formula re students and media. C*

Who are you? she texts back and in seconds she has the answer: *Cosmo. V impressed with the videos I have seen. But wondered if you're OK?*

To Cosmo: *I wasn't expecting you to be concerned. I'm fine.*

From Cosmo: *Of course, I'm concerned. Why would I not be?*

To Cosmo: *Your opinion of me makes it seem unlikely.*

From Cosmo: *Can we meet? I think we need to talk.*

To Cosmo: *No, thank you.*

From Cosmo: *A bit surprised at this cold politeness. Am I assuming too much? Are we not friends?*

To Cosmo: *That would depend on how you usually treat your friends. Standards vary.*

From Cosmo: *Please explain.*

To Cosmo: *Your comments on the news made it clear that what I thought we had in common was a figment of my imagination. Just forget about me. You were kind in the past and now you are ridiculing me in the media.*

She nearly cries; this text exchange is tormenting her. Why is he contacting her with pretend concern after what he has said to the media? She feels devastated each time she hears or reads those quotes, and they are everywhere. He has become important to her, even though she has not talked to him or seen him since he delivered her back from Plymouth, and losing his respect, not being able to trust him, is painful. But now that she has told him to forget about her, the hurt is overwhelming, it feels like loss and grief.

She has a shower, washes her hair and on a whim puts on makeup, which is not what she usually does on a school day. It is Friday and she considers going home for a visit to her parents to get away from everything that seems to be taking over her life and creating nearly constant stress.

At morning break, she turns her phone on in the staff room and sees a new message from Cosmo: Have checked media, if you refer to TV news the other day and various radio stations, they quoted comments I made two years ago in a different context. I have been contacted about the Salcombe video and told all that I have no comments to make. I am your friend. Please talk to me! I need to know you're OK, and I want to see you. I have been away at a site in New Zealand, just got back.

She goes to the staff washroom, leans against the cold tiles and tries to calm down. That she desperately wants to believe him, does not make his claim true. But after weighing up what they went through together after the TV show against what she presumed were belittling statements to the press, she decides that she has made a mistake based on how vulnerable she feels these days; hunted by the press, and alternately praised for psychic powers or derided for being a fraud depending on which side people take. I shouldn't have been so quick to assume he really said those things, she thinks, and looks at her pale face in the mirror. I do trust him, and I don't think he would say anything that would hurt me. I wasn't thinking clearly and I over-reacted.

To Cosmo: *Photographers on doorstep, voodoo dolls, publishers offering deals, anonymous letters, tabloids offering deals, school getting pissed off about media at the gates, mags offering deals, car seriously broken, lunatic fringe groups hounding me and others sending hate mail. So probably slowly losing my mind and ability to make rational judgements. Otherwise all well and feeling great. Truly sorry I misjudged you.*

From Cosmo: *Want to be rescued for the weekend? No strings.*

To Cosmo: *I like strings if they have balloons on the end.*

From Cosmo: *Is that yes or no?*

To Cosmo: *It's a yes please. But be prepared for a tantrum if I find a TV crew waiting – I'll tell them you abducted me at gunpoint.*

From Cosmo: *That sounds more like the girl I remember. I'll pick you up from your flat at 5.30 this afternoon. No need for fancy clothes. Remember the car? Black SUV, tinted windows, ready for fast exit if necessary. Keep your chin up, you're doing well, C*

'I'm going away for the weekend,' she says to Becks at the lunch break, and Becks says rudely but truthfully.

'You're kidding, right? You never go *away* - you only go home to your parents. I mean, *really*? As in going away with *a man*? And if so, who is he?'

'Yes, going away with a man, and let's just get this clear right now – I'm not telling you who he is, I only just met him. It might be a platonic but enjoyable weekend, or it might be a platonic and boring weekend, and it might involve revenge sex. Don't ask!'

Becks stares at her thoughtfully while she chews a mouthful of ham sandwich, washes it down with some coffee and she says disbelievingly, 'Revenge sex? Surely not! That's not the sort of thing you do - it sounds more like the sort of thing I would do. And who is the revenge on? I hope you're not still thinking of Harry?'

'No, I hadn't thought of him in this context - or at all. You were so right about him and I should have listened to you, as I have admitted ten times already. The revenge, if it happens, would be me having a bit of fun as a way of getting back at circumstance, chance or fate or whatever the hell it is that has put me in this dreadful situation. An act of rebellion. But it probably won't happen – as you said, it's not what I do.'

She gets up and leaves the staff room and walks around the sports field twice until it's time for class. Telling Becks has put doubt into her own mind. What is Cosmo expecting? Being friends 'with benefits' is fine, but it would be an uneven relationship, maybe making me even more vulnerable than I am already, based on how attracted I am to him. Because he has a child's little treasures in his glove compartment, and wet wipes – what could that possibly mean apart from the obvious? Is he divorced or is he married and hoping for some extra-marital fun? If that's the case I'm opting out, that would only lead to problems, particularly for me. If I get any closer to him, I might end up heartbroken – that sort of relationship never seems to work out well from what I hear and read. I'm an idiot, why did I say I would? I wish I didn't like him so much!

But despite her changeable attitude about the coming weekend, she goes home and packs a weekend bag, studies her reflection briefly in the mirror and decides to leave her hair in a ponytail. Keeping it ordinary and not looking as if she is hoping to look more attractive than when he last saw her seems like a good plan; no enticement, just stay calm and quiet and see what happens.

She resists Beck's attempts to prize out of her who the man is, and where she met him. 'Stop it! I'm saying nothing about him just now – I feel very on edge about the whole thing and talking about it is either going to make me cancel the weekend or start crying. And you can take that look off your face – it is *not* Harry! Just send a calming thought in my direction now and then, please.'

'Sure – I have actually been sending calming thoughts your way for weeks now. But you've got to promise to tell me all about it when you come back.'

At half past five she looks out the living room window and there is a black SUV with tinted windows double-parked outside. She grabs her bag, shouts 'Bye!' to Becks and runs down the stairs. She opens the rear door, chucks her bag on the seat and gets into the front, looks across at Cosmo and says 'Hi!'

'Hi, yourself,' he says and drives off, and that's all there is to it. The force field is still operational and stronger than ever; it reached her the moment she opened the passenger door, but on the surface the situation seems ordinary and mundane. Neither of them displays any sign of strong emotion; they are just two people who casually greet each other without any overt show of affection. They sit in silence for a few minutes, and she glances over at him again, studies his profile and wonders what he is thinking, and then she does something so out of character, so unexpected even to herself, that she can hardly believe it. 'Can you pull over, please? Just for a moment.'

He makes no reply, just stops behind a bus that pulls out from a bus stop.

'Are you OK?' he says, and when her hand reaches towards him, he looks properly at her face and says,

'No, you're not OK – come here.' And reaches over and pulls her towards him. The central armrest creates a wide separation between them, and their seat belts are still done up, but parts of them meet. He leans his forehead against hers, and she feels safe and realises that she has not felt like this since the night of the TV show; shielded from anything that might happen, safe inside his force field. But it is very uncomfortable, and after a minute she says, 'Sorry, I don't know why I did that,' and Cosmo moves his arm from around her shoulders and says, 'I'm not sorry, I liked it.' And she laughs and feels as if the colour has come back into the world and puts her hand on his thigh. 'I needed that.'

Chapter 23

They cross the Exe river and continue east on the road that leads to Okehampton Castle without talking. Callista sits silent and waits for whatever is to come. Cosmo has not volunteered any information about where they are going, but as they drive through Tedburn St Mary she remembers him saying that he lives somewhere near here. They emerge on the far side of Tedburn, turn into a smaller road, then a lane and finally into a tree-lined driveway with tall wrought-iron gates standing open.

Cosmo stops in front of a large two-storied brick house with too many chimneys and too many gables, a slightly overwhelming example of Victorian Gothic over-the-top-ness. Callista's mind fills with a stream of speculation and questions; is it a private residence, does Cosmo live in this huge house; but would he bring her to his home if he is married even if his wife is away? Or is it a B&B of a superior kind?

'Here we are,' he says, and he has hardly opened his door when a small girl comes running out of the front door, which vaguely resembles a church door, stops on the top step and stares at the car. Cosmo gets out and says, 'Come and say hello to our visitor, Dessi.'

Callista gets out and waits to see what will happen, but the child stays where she is and when they approach the steps up to the door, she says, "Welcome!" turns and runs at full speed into the house and disappears.

'Well, that's all you're going to get for the moment – about what I expected,' says Cosmo calmly. 'She can be very shy with new people, but she promised she would say 'welcome' – and she did, however brief her appearance was.'

'How old is she?'

'Just about to turn five. Her name is Desdemona, but we always call her Dessi.'

Callista could ask if he is divorced or a widower; the situation is still murky, and she wonders who the "we" are, but she doesn't ask; she is in a strange fatalistic state of mind, where she can wait for answers without agonizing. They walk under the peaked arch of the tall doorway, and then the hall of this bizarre house captures her full attention. She stops in the middle of the floor and looks around amazed.

Cosmo watches her face and grins. 'You don't have to be polite, feel free to comment. I know this house is a monstrosity – too big, too elaborate, too faux everything – but it's where I live with my mother and Dessi and a couple of helpers from the village. Welcome to Birdwood House, built by a forebear with more money than taste, but it's our home, so we love it.'

'I've never been in a private house with brick walls inside,' says Callista, trying to strike a safe middle path between politeness and amazement. 'And a two-story hall – like in a mansion. But that staircase is beautiful.'

Straight ahead is a branched staircase, where short, curved flights meet at a broad landing and then continue up in a single wider flight to an open gallery at the next floor.

Cosmo laughs. 'In this hideous house it is a nice surprise, isn't it? By far the best thing in the house, carved by imported Italian wood carvers when the house was built in the eighteen-seventies. You'll have time to look more closely later, but it is said that every species of bird in England is carved into those bannisters and corner posts. Dessi can waste an hour of your time later on, pointing them out. And there are some lovely fireplace surrounds in the same style here and there. But this is the only space with brickwork inside – thank God!'

They climb the stairs to the gallery at the next floor.

'We turn right here,' he says, and they continue down a wide passage, past three doors to one standing open

'Dessi decided you should have this room – she thought you would like the yellow and green colours. For obvious reasons we call it the Yellow room.'

He drops her bag on the floor and says, 'Come here' and pulls her close and she leans into him and closes her eyes and feels his hands on her back, holding her to him and they just stand there, silent and unmoving, until a small voice exclaims, 'Cosmo!' in a surprised sort of exclamation, the way people do when they unexpectedly bump into someone they like.

He lets Callista go and turns. 'Dessi!' he exclaims and grabs her under her armpits and lifts her until they are nose to nose, and they both laugh. 'This is Callista who has come for a visit, and she'd like you to show her why you wanted her to sleep in the Yellow room, if you have time to do that?'

Dessi giggles. 'Of course, silly – I always have time. You are the one who don't have time sometimes. Put me down please!'

'Quite right!' Cosmo puts her down and says causally, 'I'll leave you two to look around – Dessi knows everything, and then we'll have a drink downstairs before dinner. If you're quite sure you have time, Dessi?'

'You're teasing,' says Dessi with great dignity. 'I can

232

tell! You can go now, and we will look at everything and then we'll come down.'

'It's a very nice room,' says Callista and studies Dessi, whose brown eyes look steadily back. A skinny little girl, with wavy black hair and coffee coloured skin, dressed in jeans, a sweatshirt with a sequined red heart on the front and tiny red trainers. After a moment's scrutiny Dessi asks, 'Would you like to see the *very* best bit first or last?'

'Oh, first please,' says Callista and hopes this is the right response. 'Just in case we don't have time for the best bit, if we leave it to last.'

Dessi laughs delightedly. 'You *are* smart − Cosmo said you are.' Callista is tempted to ask what else Cosmo said about her, but it feels wrong to use a child as an unwitting informer.

Dessi walks over to one of the windows. 'Come over here - look!' She pulls on a cord and the curtains glide smoothly together until they meet in the middle. 'Isn't that great? Would you like to try?'

'I'd love to try.' She joins Dessi beside the window and they take turns pulling the curtains open and shut.

'The second-best thing is the big cupboard, see − you open the door like this.' Dessi reaches up, holds the wrought-iron lever down and hangs her weight from it to open the door to the huge oak cupboard. 'See, lots of drawers on one side.' She points. 'And − look!

Another door! A cupboard inside a cupboard – isn't that great?'

The interior of the cupboard is divided into two equal halves, on one side is a row of deep drawers and on the other five shelves at the bottom and at the top a door with a key in it.

'Open it!' orders Callista's small guide. 'I can't reach, and I'm not allowed on the chairs with my shoes on. See those little drawers in there? Some rich person kept special things there and money, maybe they had gold and diamonds. And then they locked that little door so nobody could steal things. But there's nothing left - Cosmo and I had a look, and all the drawers are empty.'

Callista says gravely, 'That's a pity! It would have been exciting to find some treasure. Do you think we should go downstairs now?'

'I do – Cosmo likes me to come and talk to him and Grandma for a while before dinner – so they don't get bored just talking to each other, you understand.'

She takes Callista's hand and leads her down the long hallway to the gallery where it opens up above the hall and stops.

'This is another special thing,' says Dessi seriously, 'and it's quite unusual, I don't know anyone else who has a high room like this. If you drop things from here, they usually break.'

Callista tries to keep a straight face. 'What kind of things do, eh ... people drop from here?'

'It's usually me,' says Dessi in a fit of honesty. 'I've dropped a couple of things, well, perhaps three or four. When I was younger, you know? Just to see what would happen.'

Halfway down, on the landing where the stairs separate into two flights, Dessi stops. 'You know Cosmo? Well, people usually think he's my daddy - do you think that?'

'I don't know,' says Callista. 'Is he not your Dad?'

'No, he's my nuncle, but he's instead of a dad, because I haven't got one. I've been with him since I was a baby. He's my best friend, and then after that I like the Joans best, and Grandma, of course – no sorry, she comes after Cosmo. Let's go down.'

Chapter 24

They walk into a large living room where Cosmo is standing by a window talking to a woman sitting in an armchair. He turns when they come in and holds his hand out. 'Come and meet my mother, Callista.'

The woman in the chair is grey haired and very thin and there are two walking sticks leaning against one side of her chair. 'It's a pleasure to meet you,' she says and Callista gets the impression that she is being scrutinized with unusual focus. 'I've seen you on the internet and on TV but ...'

Now Cosmo has noticed too and looks from his mother to Callista and back again with a frown. 'But what, mother? Explain please, Callista is getting embarrassed.'

Mrs. St Clair continues to study Callista's face for a

moment and then she smiles. 'I beg your pardon, that was very rude! But the likeness to someone I used to know is more than a likeness, it's like seeing her again. A girl I went to boarding school with - we were best friends for years, but she died young – and you are the spitting image. What's your surname, Callista?'

'Bannister,' says Callista with a feeling of slight apprehension. The situation is unusual and before she can make up her mind about what to say next, Dessi interrupts. 'Was your friend pretty too? As pretty as Callista?'

'Darling, she was exactly the same, exactly! It's uncanny – I thought the likeness was astonishing when I saw you on that TV show with Cosmo, but it's even more pronounced in real life, it makes me feel very sentimental - I was devastated when Virginia died.'

Cosmo breaks the spell by asking Callista what she wants to drink and pours her a glass of wine.

'We nearly always have a drink before dinner,' he says and gestures to the chair beside his mother's. 'Have a seat and if Dessi has time, she'll offer you some of those nice little things that Joan made before she went home.'

He sits down on the far side of his mother and Dessi gives him a look, but she brings a little tray from the table and offers it around.

'I didn't know she was called Virginia,' he says to his mother. 'You've talked about her once or twice, but

I don't think I knew her name. Did you name our Ginny Virginia after her?'

'My mother? Is her name Virginia? I thought she was called Ginny.'

'It's just a short version, like you're really called Desdemona, but we always call you Dessi.'

Dessi turns to Callista. 'You haven't met her probably. I go and see her now and then with Cosmo and Grandma– she's in a place, because she doesn't talk or walk, and she can't look after me.'

'It's called a care home,' says Cosmo and manages to hold his glass out of the way as Dessi climbs onto his lap and squirms around to face Callista. 'Sit still, Dessi or I'll spill my wine.'

He turns to Callista who sits quietly waiting for someone to break away from the topic of Dessi's mother, who is in a care home and start a different subject; she doesn't feel that she should do it.

'Ginny was a drug user and she either overdosed or used something that was contaminated. She had a series of strokes that destroyed her. So I'm Dessi's guardian and she's been living here since she was five months old.'

'No, you're not!' says Dessi. 'You're my nuncle, don't tell fibs or Grandma will tell you off.'

It takes some time to explain to Dessi that you can be both an uncle and a guardian, and all the time Callista is aware of Mrs. St Clair's eyes on her and begins to feel slightly unnerved by the constant attention.

They have dinner in a large kitchen at a big deal table with scratches and gouges from generations of use. Someone has prepared everything and left it ready on low heat, and she wonders if one of the helpers Cosmo mentioned also prepares dinner. After a beef casserole with roasted vegetables and ice cream with chocolate sauce, Cosmo goes upstairs to put Dessi to bed and Callista follows slowly behind Mrs. St Clair to the living room, carrying their coffee cups and a thermos on a tray.

'Arthritis keeps me prisoner,' says Mrs. St Clair when she is settled into her armchair again. 'It's a curse, but at least I have the blessing of Cosmo and Dessi living here with me. Without them and some help from the village I couldn't have stayed here.'

She casts a glance at Callista, as if she's assessing how she is reacting, and Callista feels certain that what is coming is some kind of test.

'When my husband died about ten years ago – he was a lot older than me – Cosmo sold his apartment in Plymouth and moved back to Birdwood. And then of course we had the tragedy with Ginny taking drugs, which we didn't know about until that hideous overdose, just devastating. When that happened and she had those strokes, she was just getting quite well-known as an actress, a stage actress, after years of only getting minor roles, and we were so pleased for her. Cosmo did everything, got legal guardianship of Dessi and hired a young woman with one little child to live here for a couple of years to help with Dessi, so he could work. I'm sure you know that his job means he's often away for a week or two on sites – sometimes more. But it's all worked out so well! And for me it's lovely to be able to stay in this house – I have lived here for forty-six years, ever since I married.'

Callista makes some suitable comments and hopes that Cosmo will soon return from upstairs. The feeling of being closely studied has not ceased, it sits behind everything they talk about and makes the conversation hard work.

I can't work out why she's so obsessed with the likeness, she thinks, and listens with one ear to Mrs. St Clair's reminiscing about Dessi's first couple of years and descriptions of all the funny and clever things she says and does. She must have had a very close friendship with her friend Ginny, but I can't be the exact copy of her, she must be exaggerating or time has dulled the memory.

When Cosmo returns, she tries to change the subject by asking how many stories he had to read, and he laughs. 'No, just one story, but several times. We read it every night, four times tonight. We're working our way through mine and Ginny's childhood books, and at the moment she's obsessed with The Little Digger – she knows it by heart.'

'Cosmo, could you get the green photo album out from the shelf behind me? I'm sure it's still there,' says Mrs. St Clair. 'The fat one that's usually at the very bottom of the pile – I haven't looked at it for years. I want to show Callista something.'

He finds the album and puts it on his mother's lap and after a couple of minutes of turning pages she says, 'Yes – here it is! I was sure I remembered at least a couple of pages of photos from her twenty-first birthday, just a year before she died – that was in nineteen-seventy-two.'

She hands the album to Callista. 'Have a look and see if you don't think the likeness to you is extraordinary.'

Cosmo crouches beside her chair and Callista sits stunned, hardly breathing as her eyes go back and forth between the two pages full of photos. Groups of people, couples, people making speeches, a table laden with gifts – and in nearly every single photo a girl who could be herself. It makes her feel claustrophobic in a new way, and Cosmo puts his warm hand over hers where she holds the side of the album so that hard her knuckles are white. 'Incredible,' he says and looks across at his mother. 'They could be twins! Now I

241

understand why you were so stunned when Callista walked in.'

His gaze moves to Callista's face. 'Are you all right? Did it spook you to find you had a double?'

Instead of responding she turns to Mrs. St Clair. 'That tall boy beside Ginny in those family groups – is that her brother? They are very alike.'

Cosmo gets to his feet, takes the album across to his mother again and puts it open on her lap and she looks down and smiles. 'That's Anthony,' she says. 'Ginny's older brother – he was such a lovely boy! I never had a brother and he used to treat Ginny and me as if we were both his sisters. Anthony got quite famous, you know - you might have heard of him, he is Sir Anthony Williams now. He retired recently, well in the last couple of years anyway – he was a well-known conductor.'

She drinks some of her coffee and continues before Callista can think of anything to say, 'We didn't stay in touch, but every now and then over the years we'd meet up at some party or event and talk for a while - but he never seemed to need old friendships the way most of us do, so meeting him always left me feeling a little disappointed. Perhaps I reminded him too much of Ginny and made him uncomfortable. Or else he had simply moved on, as my husband used to say, when I complained about how remote Anthony always seemed.'

Callista says goodnight just after ten and goes upstairs, leaving Cosmo to turn off lights and lock doors once his mother has retired to her bedroom.

In the yellow room, Callista turns on the bedside light and sits in the armchair beside the fireplace in the dim light that suits her mood and considers this nearly unbelievable coincidence and wonders if it means something. My life has taken such a strange turn, she thinks. All these things that seem dreamlike – or maybe nightmarish – where has it all come from? Ever since Salcombe, the only time I have really felt completely safe and kind of insulated from the strangeness, shielded from it, was in the lift when I suddenly came out of the claustrophobia episode. I haven't felt totally safe for one single moment, not a single one, apart from with Cosmo, since those words entered my head in Salcombe a year ago, and the car crashed into the shop.

Chapter 25

Callista pulls the curtains over the two windows, but she doesn't feel like going to bed. There is too much going on in her head and she looks indecisively around the room. What a huge room this is, but probably a hundred and fifty years ago people who could afford a house like this expected at least the main bedrooms to be like this with room for a sofa and an armchair in front of a fireplace. And how cosy this room will be on a winter evening with a fire in the grate. Bet the mantlepiece and the shelves above it were carved by those Italian carvers, they are gorgeous, vines and bunches of grapes and birds. I think I love Cosmo, well I do, I think I fell in love with him even before I talked to him. That's why it was so hurtful when I thought he was dismissing me as a silly woman, when I thought for a while that he didn't believe what I said after all. If I tell Mrs. St Claire that Anthony is my biological father, will she be shocked – even if I don't mention that my mother had sex with him?

She laughs to herself at the thought of coolly saying at the breakfast table, 'And by the way, my mother had sex with Sir Anthony, so I suppose that explains the likeness.'

Not that I would ever tell her that! No, of course she wouldn't be shocked, she must have been young in the late sixties and seventies, when everyone started taking the pill and girls could have sex without worrying about getting pregnant, and the hippie era was full-on and Carnaby Street and all that. I think she'd be pretty un-shockable. But I need to do the right thing, and if I don't tell her now, and if this thing with Cosmo develops, and then I tell her much later, after we've met several times, then it might seem strange to her - that I said nothing earlier. And I feel she deserves to know, because it would be a link to Ginny, and she obviously loved her and misses her still after all these decades - her best friend who has never been replaced. So not telling her would be unkind when it's such a simple thing to do.

She gets undressed, pulls on a T-shirt and sits down on the little sofa, which is cushiony and soft, curls her feet under her and tries to imagine the best way to tell Mrs.

St Clair, what words she might use and how to introduce the subject. When there is a knock on the door half an hour later, she is still deep in thought imagining the conversation they would have and what questions Mrs. St Clair might ask. For a moment she considers pretending to be asleep, but only for a moment, then temptation wins. She gets up and says, 'come in' and Cosmo opens the door and stands there, looking at her in way she can't interpret.

'Would you come in properly, please' she says. 'And close the door - I've only got a T-shirt and panties on.'

He chuckles but obeys and closes the door. 'Mother can't get up the stairs and Dessi is sound asleep – and Joan went home at six. Nobody but me can see you.'

'I don't know what to do!' It bursts out of her; she hesitates about where to start, how to explain this strange confluence of other people's lives that has culminated in this particular moment in her own life, and which has made her feel so indecisive. Cosmo walks across to the sofa, wraps his arms around her and says calmly, 'What's the problem? Something about that earlier Virginia really got to you – I could see it, but why? Was it just the incredible likeness? Or was it something my mother said?'

'You know I told you that I got an anonymous letter? That's where this starts, but it's a long story. I want to tell you - if you have time?'

He laughs, 'That damned thing is catching. Dessi

loves it for some reason, it takes on new forms every day. Shall we sit down?'

She is silent for so long that he holds her away to look at her face. 'If it's a long story, I mean – perhaps we should sit down, if it's going to take some time.'

'Let's sit on the sofa,' she says, determined not to say something ridiculous and needy like 'don't let me go' which would make her sound like a twit in a soppy novel.

'Sounds like a nice place to sit,' he says and she can hear the smile. 'And then you can tell me what this is about. I'm sure it's nowhere near as problematic as you imagine.

He's always so calm, she thinks with an inward smile, he never seems to panic or get caught up in rushed thoughts, he's like a rock, he lets things flow around him.

'Now then - tell me!' he says when they sit down on the sofa. He puts his arm around her shoulders and pulls her close. 'Are you warm enough?'

She leans into him and smiles, 'Now I am, you're lovely and warm.' The sound of his breathing, the warmth from his body and the feel of his arm creates that strange feeling again. It is as if she is now inside that field of energy that surrounds him, just like in the lift, and she thinks how weird it is, unlike anything she has experienced with anyone else, and how she knew from the moment she first met him that she was being pulled towards him. He makes her feel safe, not just physically, but mentally, and she feels that she can say and do anything at all, and there will be no judgment, no repercussions.

She tells him the whole saga about how her parents discovered her father was sterile, how Anthony lectured at the school of music and how he agreed to be the so-called donor, not via a turkey baster, but by Callista's mother having sex with him. She gets up and finds her phone and returns to the sofa, hands him the phone with the photo of the anonymous letter on the screen and waits for his reaction.

'So, you do understand, don't you, that I must either tell her now, I don't mean tonight, but this weekend, or not at all.' The unspoken implications that she is coming back, and that this is something on-going is not wasted on Cosmo, who pulls her closer and leans his head against hers.

'And how did you get this letter? Was it delivered or sent by mail?'

'It was couriered to the school, no sender's name. I have no idea who sent it and I don't really care. But I do worry that whoever wrote it might send something to the press or call them.'

Cosmo straightens her up and turns his head to look at her with a hint of a smile. 'Is this what you're worried about? And if it is, why? It's a perfectly simple choice that only you can make – either you let my mother continue to forever regard this as an incredible, coincidental likeness, that she will talk about every time she sees you – or you tell her what you just told me, or most of it, and she will regard you as very special, decide you've been sent by fate to brighten her days and never let you go home again. And if you're going to tell her, you are right - you should do it this weekend.'

'Cosmo, would you please come to bed with me – if you have time?'

'I thought you'd never ask,' he says. 'My time is yours.'

Much later, they lie spooned and sleepy in Callista's bed, and she says drowsily, 'I was hoping there would be a balloon on the end of the string.' And Cosmo pulls her back against his chest and says something so softly into the back of her head that she can't hear more than a couple of words and knows that she's not meant to hear, so she makes no reply.

They wake in the morning to the sound of Dessi exclaiming 'Cosmo!' with more surprised gusto than ever. She stands like a miniature sentinel beside the bed on Callista's side balancing a book on top of her head with one hand, smiling widely.

'I thought I would let Callista read my morning

story instead of you,' she says. 'As a treat for her, you know - but you're both here, isn't that great!'

She clambers over Callista and wriggles down between them, and exclaims, 'Cosmo! You haven't got your PJ pants on. Don't look at him, Callista, and I'll run and get them.'

She leaves them laughing and Callista says, 'Now she'll tell everyone that she found us in the same bed, and you had nothing on! I'd better get up and put my T-shirt on at least.'

'Here it is,' says Cosmo and reaches up to the bedhead. 'I chucked it up there last night.'

Dessi orders Cosmo to put his pants on under the covers, gets back into the bed between them and leans her head against Callista. 'Please read me this story,' she says and reaches for the book. 'It's a new one, I'm sick of The Little Digger book. I like leaning on you, Callista, you're like little soft cushions for my head.'

Chapter 26

On the way downstairs, Cosmo says, 'My mother doesn't get up for breakfast. It takes her a long time to get going in the morning, she gets a lot of pain at night for some reason and can't sleep, so whichever Joan is here gives her breakfast in bed, and she usually emerges about lunchtime. Having a shower and getting dressed is a slow process. Dessi helps – she runs around and finds the right shoes and the right jumper and helps her put her socks on, very useful.'

Callista laughs when she realises what he just said. 'Are there two women called Joan? Dessi talked about the Joans last night, and I thought it was the surname Jones– how funny!'

'The senior Joan, who is here this morning, and her niece - also called Joan. They divide the week between them as it suits them and as it fits with other commitments they have. I must have seven-day cover for when I'm away on a site, and I'm not a great cook, so they always prepare a meal before they go home. There's also a cousin of the younger Joan who has offered to step in if the two Joans should happen to be busy at the same time.'

'Isn't it lucky this house had a bedroom for your mother downstairs,' says Callista as they walk across the brick floor of the hall towards the kitchen at the far end of the wing. 'I didn't think houses from this era did, apart from possibly a housekeeper's room tucked away behind the kitchen.'

'We converted the so-called breakfast room two years ago – plenty of space to make it into a bed-cum-sitting room with a bathroom. We never used it anyway, and she needs to be on the ground floor. You might like Dessi to take you on a tour upstairs later, she loves being useful, and I've got to take a call from New Zealand at half past nine – they're calling about another potential job there, but I might not take it.'

She asks no questions, the few words she heard spoken softly against the back of her head last night are running through her mind; she will wait for further developments, secure in the knowledge of what she heard.

. . .

In the kitchen Cosmo introduces Joan and within a minute he is laughing without a trace of embarrassment, 'OK, Joan – I can see the not-so-secret glee there – it's as clear as daylight! Obviously Dessi has told you about finding me in Callista's bed this morning – I hope you're not shocked.'

And they both laugh while Callista looks on and wonders at the kind of relationships that seem natural to Cosmo, something engendered by his calm strength and kindness, and she wonders if he has any idea how different he is from most other men.

After breakfast, while Cosmo goes to talk to someone in New Zealand in the room Dessi refers to as the small study, she and Callista go upstairs and make their beds together, before Dessi conducts the tour of the upper floor.

'You've got the best room after Grandma's old room,' she says. 'Her old room is the biggest bedroom in the whole house – well, upstairs anyway - and it's got four windows because it's on a corner and Cosmo was going to put you there because it has a lovely new bathroom – but I wanted you to be in the yellow room because of how you can pull the curtains that special way, it's the only room with that. Do you love Cosmo?'

Caught by surprise, Callista says nothing for a moment and Dessi continues, 'Joan says you probably love each other, or you wouldn't sleep in the same bed, it's like a special rule for adults – I didn't know that. I told Grandma when I went to help her with some stuff this morning and she said she thinks you love each other, because Cosmo looks at you in a funny way, she noticed last night. And here is the last bedroom, this is the ugly one, it's grey and pink – yuk! Do you want to see my secret?'

She leads Callista along the corridor and looks carefully both ways before she opens a door between two bedrooms. 'We have to be *very* quiet up here, OK?'

The wooden stairs are steep; Dessi goes first and whispers over her shoulder, 'Now, you close the door behind us! And put your feet where I put mine, OK? It squeaks if you put your foot in the middle.'

Callista follows her guide slowly, setting her feet carefully just along the wall and Dessi whispers, 'No loud talking up here – you have to whisper.'

She opens the door at the top and Callista follows her into a vast and dimly lit space with thick square-cut beams supporting the roof and six narrow dormer windows covered with dust. Dessi stands on tiptoes and flicks a light switch and a single lamp hanging from a cord adds minimal illumination.

To the left of the door is a huge trestle table with sheets draped over it, and Dessi points and says, 'Guess!' in an excited whisper.

There are shapes under the cloth and Callista thinks she knows what it is, but she whispers back,

'Heavens, Dessi! What a strange thing – is it a big dinner table all set out with glasses and plates?'

'No! Help me – I *can* do it on my own, but I have to run right around and lift it carefully, so if you help it will be quicker. We'll do one side each.'

Lifting half the cover and folding it back reveals a large model railway installation with tunnels and bridges and a town with a station.

'There's a village and two farms at the other end that we can't see, they're under the cover at that end,' says Dessi, still in a whisper. 'With tiny sheep and things, and little pigs. Look at the little people – and see those tiny cars on the road? Isn't it great?'

'It's lovely, the best railway I've ever seen. Why are we whispering?'

Dessi beckons Callista to bend down and says quietly. 'I don't want Cosmo to hear us. This is a secret - he doesn't know it's here. But one day soon I'll show him, and it will be a huge surprise! I'm saving it for his birthday, isn't that a great present?'

After tiptoeing down the attic stairs and quietly opening the door just a crack, so Dessi can check there is nobody in the hallway, they go down to the ground floor and meet Cosmo on his way to look for them.

'What have you two been doing?' he says and Dessi says airily, 'Oh, just housework – you know, making beds and tidying up. Is Grandma up yet?'

'I don't know – I've just finished talking to the man

in Christchurch, and I haven't been to see her yet. And I'm sorry, but I have to lock myself in again for half an hour or so and send an email with some suggestions to this chap in New Zealand so he can put a proposal together over the weekend and present it at a meeting on Monday. Can you two entertain yourselves?'

'Of course!' says Dessi. 'We'll see you when you have time. Callista and I can make some plans for things we can do today.' She turns to Callista. 'We'll start with Joan, so we can find out if Grandma is ready for visitors yet. She'll know.'

Chapter 27

Joan is loading the dishwasher and putting breakfast things away. 'No, Mrs. St Clair isn't up yet, she said she'll stay in bed a while longer. And don't you go in and disturb her, Dessi – she might have a snooze. She didn't sleep well last night, and it would do her good. Would you like a cup of tea, Miss Bannister? I've just put the kettle on the AGA.'

'You should call her Callista!' says Dessi. 'That's her *real* name. And can I please have a cup of tea too, seeing it's the weekend and we have a visitor?'

They sit side by side at the table with their cups of tea, Dessi's more milk than tea, and watch Joan as she moves between the table, the bench and pantry.

'I'm not here all day when Cosmo is at home,' she says over her shoulder and disappears into a pantry big enough to be a bedroom. 'I come in the morning and

257

make breakfast and help Mrs. St Clair with whatever she needs.'

She emerges with a packet of macaroni and a tin of something under her arm and heads for the fridge. 'And then I prepare the evening meal, and sometimes I make something for lunch. I share the job with my niece – she's Joan too - one of us is always available and we just organise it between us. Adele comes in two days a week and does the cleaning, and Cosmo heats up the supper at night. Dessi's very good at helping her grandmother with little things in the morning too, aren't you, Dessi? She and I make the beds together first thing after breakfast usually, but I think you've already done it today?'

'We did it together,' says Dessi. 'But Callista didn't know hospital corners, so I had to show her. I thought everyone knew that!'

Callista watches Joan as she gets more things out and puts them on the kitchen bench beside the stove. She's preparing two meals at once, she thinks, she's so used to doing it that she doesn't even have to think – she can talk and keep track of what she needs at the same time. I wonder what Cosmo told her about me. I could see she knew all about me when he introduced me, the way her eyes ran over me, assessing me. Or that might have been because Dessi had told her about finding us in bed together. But she seems friendly.

'Callista isn't magic, you know,' says Dessi. 'Cosmo

says those things she did are very special, but it's not magic, like she's not a fairy or like someone in a story. And can I please do the cheese again? Is it for lunch?'

'Macaroni cheese for lunch and chicken for supper,' says Joan and puts a grater and a chopping board on the table. 'Come over this side, Dessi and you can grate the cheese – just remember how to hold it! And yes, I know Callista isn't magic.'

She smiles at Callista, who can't make up her mind whether she should provide some sort of comment or just wait for what's to come next.

'And what is it you do?' asks Joan and turns back to the stove. 'For a job I mean'

Callista laughs. 'You mean when I'm not busy being special, but not quite magic? I teach at St Michael's high school in Exeter - science and maths.'

'I saw you on TV – and I knew right away you weren't one of those crazy people who call the police and say they know where bodies are buried and all that sort of thing. I said to Dylan - that's my son, who lives with me though he's plenty old enough to go and find a place for himself – I said to Dylan that I could tell right away that you were a reasoning kind of person, clever.'

She smiles across the table and moves Dessi's hand with the grater into the middle of the chopping board. 'Not too close to the edge, or the cheese will be on the floor. And it was really good the way you kept that Ronald in check – I enjoyed that! He's a tricky customer, but you didn't let him get away with anything. And Mrs. St Clair said exactly the same thing the next day, she thought you were very clever the way you handled yourself.'

'It was quite difficult sitting there with those strong lights on me and trying to deal with his questions without letting him get the upper hand.'

'I saw it too,' says Dessi, who has put the grater to one side and is eating the grated cheese. 'You had lovely boots on, with chains – did you bring them? Can I try them on and then you can take a photo of me with them on? If you have time?'

'I'll bring them next time,' says Callista without thinking and sees Joan smile as she lifts Dessi from the chair.

'Thanks for doing that, Dessi - but that cheese is for the sauce. I'll cut you a piece of cheese to eat.'

They have lunch in the kitchen, which is lovely and warm with the old AGA radiating heat from its cast iron heart. Cosmo takes the macaroni cheese casserole out of the warming oven and puts it on the table, and Dessi picks up her knife and fork in anticipation.

Mrs. St Clair, who seems more mobile today than she was yesterday and walked to the kitchen at a nearly normal speed, says, 'Dessi – remember your manners!' Dessi lowers the cutlery that has been pointing straight up in her little hands. 'Sorry, I forgot!'

Callista observes their interactions throughout lunch; Mrs. St Clair talks as much to Dessi as to the adults, Cosmo leaves most of the table discipline to his mother and Dessi seems used to the process, chats to Cosmo and Callista, and tells her grandmother about her plans for the day. They are using the multi-generational environment to great effect, thinks Callista, and listens to Dessi asking her grandmother if she is allowed to get down, before the others have finished.

'You may,' says Mrs. St Clair and Dessi slides off her chair and takes her plate and glass to the kitchen bench.

'I'll go and see if there are any eggs,' she says and leaves by the door at the other end of the kitchen, and Cosmo says, 'I'll show you the gardens when we've had coffee, Callista. Are you happy to have coffee here Mother or would you like it in the living room?'

'In the living room, I think – I need my good chair.' She turns to Callista and says in explanation, 'At the moment I like my armchair in there better than any other chair in the house, it suits my back, and we always keep the heating on in that smaller living room – I get cold because I sit still so much.'

She gets up with some effort, picks up her walking sticks and sets out for the living room, leaving Cosmo and Callista alone for the first time since early that morning.

'Come here, you,' says Cosmo and puts his arms around her. 'I think we have time for a quick hug before we make coffee.'

'I'm going to tell your mother about Anthony. Should I do it when Dessi is around or not?'

'Any way you want – Dessi might like to know later on that she was present when you told my mother. It's a kind of historical event, don't you think?'

'OK, I'll do it when we're all in the living room. Did you mother just say, "the little living room" – is there an even bigger one?'

'Oh God yes – you haven't seen half of the ground floor yet. I forgot to take you around before lunch. There's a huge and hideously formal living room that we never use, an equally formal dining room with table that sits sixteen or so, that we also never use and then the big study, which is like a library-cum office that my industrious forebears used - full of books that nobody reads. Then there's the room called "the ladies' withdrawing room" that my mother used when I was a child – you know, when her friends called in for coffee and things like that, it's actually a lovely room, nice and sunny. I can't remember when we last used it, possible about ten years ago and I have no idea why my mother stopped using it. The place is a bit like a museum in some respects. But we heat only the rooms we use and the hall, and the AGA keeps the kitchen warm. Sometimes I think we're mad living here in this vast place, but it's home and always has been.'

'My room was lovely and warm – I didn't realise the radiator was on. Do they stay on all the year round – in the rooms you use, I mean?'

'We usually turn them on in September. This house gets very cold even early in autumn if we don't, and I turned the heating on a couple of weeks ago. Mother's room is always warm, we have electric panel heaters there.'

It must cost a fortune, she thinks while she wipes the table, to keep this vast house maintained and heated and the gardens tidy and paying staff. Either someone has income from invested money or Cosmo earns far more than I thought geologists would earn, but no, surely not enough for this place. I hope to goodness his mother doesn't think I'm after their money or something. Not that I would mind marrying someone who had pots of money, I mean, who would? But to be suspected of having ulterior motives, no thanks!

They load a tray and are about to leave the kitchen, when Dessi returns with a little basket, looking excited.

'Wellies off!' says Cosmo and Dessi kicks her boots off. 'I'll put them in the boot room in a minute, I just want to show you this first. See? Two more than yesterday, six! Isn't that great?'

'Excellent,' says Cosmo. 'Come on down to the living room when you've put your boots away and you can have some of those chocolate fingers you like – I got them out to have with our coffee. And remember to wash your hands.'

Chapter 28

When they are all sitting down in the living room with Dessi on Cosmo's knee, he says, 'Mother, Callista has something to tell you, which I think will surprise you.'

'Oh no!' exclaims Dessi. 'Not my *secret*! Please don't tell them!'

'No, of course not, Dessi!' says Callista. 'I would *never* tell your secret to anyone, that's something only you can do.'

She gathers her thoughts and tries to remember how she had planned to broach the subject and fails, so she jumps straight in.

'When I asked you last night who that young man in the photos was, you said he was Ginny's older brother Anthony. And I have just very recently found out that he is my biological father.'

265

To Callista's surprise Mrs. St Clair's doesn't look surprised, but triumphant. She says nothing, just looks expectantly at Callista.

'I'll tell you how I found out,' she continues, hoping this is not going to lead to a negative reaction of some kind. 'I got an anonymous letter after all the publicity, and the person who wrote it told me that Anthony is my biological father, just that, nothing more. My mother told me the rest, that they couldn't have a child, because my Dad had mumps and was sterile. He is a cellist and he studied music at the music school where Anthony was a teacher – I think they got on well, though they were more than twenty years apart in age. Anthony offered to donate sperm – and the result is me. And it explains, of course, why you saw such a strong likeness to Virginia, that family likeness those two shared.'

Dessi looks from Callista to her grandmother and back again, not comprehending the facts, but aware of the tension in the room, and Mrs. St Clair exclaims triumphantly, 'I knew it! I *knew* it couldn't just be coincidence – it was uncanny, like seeing Ginny again, even some of your mannerisms – the way you play with a strand of hair with your left hand, wind it around your forefinger. I'd never thought of it, but the moment I saw you doing it, I recognized it as one of Ginny's trademarks. I lay awake for hours last night trying to think how it could be, and I did wonder if maybe

Anthony had a baby with someone he didn't marry, but I didn't dare ask you, of course, in case you didn't know anything about it.'

Dessi slides off Cosmo's lap and disappears out the door while he says calmly, 'So the original Ginny would have been Callista's aunt if she hadn't died so young. What did she die of?'

'She got bacterial meningitis and died within a week. Nobody knew how she got it - I believe it's very rare. These days they would have tested everyone she knew, and we would all have been put on antibiotics, and everyone we had been in contact with would be traced - fifty years ago things weren't quite so organised, but nobody else in our group of friends got it. Such a tragedy, she was my very best friend and I never made another friend like her. Have you met Anthony?'

'I literally only just found out – until I got that anonymous letter, I didn't even know my Dad wasn't my biological father. But I've never met him, no.'

Callista hopes that Mrs. St Clair won't ask to see the letter. That bit about Anthony being mad might upset her, but before she can make up her mind to lie and say she threw it away, Cosmo intervenes. 'Callista can show you the letter. She has a photo of it on her phone.'

So Callista gets her phone out of her back pocket, finds the image, and hands the phone to Mrs. St Clair, who reads the letter and nods. 'I suppose the person who wrote it refers to all those crazy things Anthony seems to have become involved in as he's got older. He blogs a lot these days about all kind of things, and he seems to be very active on social media – not that I follow him, but I see things he writes on Facebook sometimes. He is friends with quite a few people I know, so now and then something pops up on my newsfeed, things he has commented on, and I get to see what he's interested in – and it's mostly a bit mad, way beyond what most of us regard as normal.' She makes a face of disgust. 'The other day it was about poltergeists in some house in Dorset he wants the Historical Places Trust to buy, the house isn't of value, but he thinks the ghosts are – the HPT will be squirming with embarrassment to have one of their prominent fund raisers being serious about preserving ghosts.'

'They might like it - maybe it will give them some extra publicity,' says Cosmo. 'They might get donations from a whole new tranche of people now.'

Mrs. St Clair shakes her head, still thinking of her old friend and his strange interests. 'I'll tell you another thing he believes in – those so-called lay lines that are supposed to connect the stone circles – some kind of cosmic energy lines, or maybe they're supposed to be magnetic lines. Perhaps he was into all these things when he was a student too – we were part of that generation, ban the bomb, vegetarians, free love, the whole thing. He was just that much older than Ginny and me that we didn't mix with his friends, so I'm only guessing. But he used to smoke pot behind the garage with his friends - it was that era.' She laughs at the memory of her younger self. 'Not me, I was always too scared to try in case my parents found out. I didn't have a rebellious bone in my body in those days. I find it hard to believe how obedient I was – I'm far more liberal about things now that I'm decades older. Quite funny!'

Cosmo shakes his head and says decisively, 'If the relationship becomes known it will increase the media interest exponentially. I hope he won't take it into his head to make it public himself – you'd have to go into hiding, Callista.'

The thought makes Callista shiver. 'Imagine the speculation and the headlines, unbearable! It's bad enough now with people thinking I have all kinds of mystical powers and wanting me to subject myself to experiments and help them find things they have lost – including bodies.'

But Mrs. St Clair shrugs. 'It will wear off - these things always do. And it's not likely you'll have one of those experiences again, is it? Statistically, I mean. How many times in a lifetime can you expect to be within earshot – if that's the term – of someone who is at that very moment about to kill someone? The odds against any given person being in that situation even *once* in their life must be astronomical – apart from in war situations, of course.'

And in Callista's mind something changes, she feels her sense of logic and proportion change gears and run more smoothly, worry and apprehension slide away. She feels lighter, more relaxed about what has happened than she has since the incident in Salcombe, and she smiles at Mrs. St Clair. 'Thank you for that thought Mrs. St Clair! I can't imagine why I never thought of that angle myself – and I'm usually logical and work things out.'

'I'm not surprised – you were right in the middle of it and with all the things that have happened since, the media and everything, you probably haven't been your usual rational self. And please call me Louise – much easier.'

Cosmo looks searchingly at Callista with a slight frown. 'Did you never think of it in those terms? Have you gone around for weeks worrying that it would keep happening? I had no idea! I know you worried that something was wrong with your brain, but that's another aspect of it. I should have messaged you when the Salcombe video came out – my first thought was that if you've experienced it twice, it wouldn't happen to you again in a thousand years, so to speak.'

'I know. It makes sense from that point of view,' says Callista thoughtfully. 'And that's great, of course, a huge relief. But how and why did it happen at all? What is it about my mind that enables the thoughts of others to come through like spoken words inside my head?'

Cosmo smiles across at her. 'I think you *do* have something, a sensor of some kind, that enables you to pick up thoughts of a particular kind from someone else's mind, someone who is physically close when they think thoughts about immediate violence or about killing. You've never felt any other thoughts invade your mind, have you?'

'No, never.'

'Well then, that's all good then' says Mrs. St Clair, who seems to casually accept that Callista has specialist extra-sensory powers that have twice prevented people being killed. 'Off you go and show Callista things while it's still nice and sunny, Cosmo. The forecast is for showers later on. Where did Dessi go?'

'I think she got bored,' says Cosmo and gets up. 'Well take the cups to the kitchen and go for a walk and see if we can find her, she's sure to be outside.'

'We'll go out through the back door,' he says and puts their cups on the kitchen bench. 'You've got sneakers on, and I'll put on my wellies in the boot room, come on!'

Callista stands on the stone slab floor in the boot

room behind the kitchen and thinks absentmindedly that she has read about boot rooms and breakfast rooms, but she's never been in a house of this kind, where those things are taken for granted, used by generations and still called by the traditional names. It is interesting to speculate on all the hundreds of outdoor shoes, and wellies and maybe even clogs that have been left here before their owners continued into the kitchen. An invisible history of those who have lived and worked here.

'Coming?' Cosmo holds the door open and adds. 'I could see you were surprised at what my mother said. She's said all along that she completely believes you – she watched the TV show and the next morning she said she was pleased I had diverted some of the probing questions that Ronald launched at you – she said you deserved a bit of help and it was obvious you were clever and level-headed, and if you said it happened, then we must believe it.'

'She is an amazing woman - just great, as Dessi would say.' Callista walks ahead of him out the door into a large vegetable garden with a hen coop set further back.

'Dessi! Where are you?' calls Cosmo and Callista thinks how lucky Dessi is to live here, where the adults don't panic if they don't see her, where a not-quite-five-year-old can come and go as she likes and the adults just go outside and call for her if they want to talk to her.

'Coming!' comes Dessi's voice from some distance away. 'No, wait - you come here! I found some new poo!'

Behind the hencoop is a large field of tall grass and halfway across it Dessi crouches with her back to them.

'Could be anything,' says Cosmo as they walk towards her. 'She loves poos. Watch out for holes, there are rabbit burrows here.'

'Look!' Dessi points at something just in front of her. 'Do you think it's a fox? Or a wolf?'

Cosmo grins at Callista before he crouches down beside Dessi, 'I'm not sure, I think probably a fox. Come and have a look, Callista.'

Of all the unlikely activities after a first night spent in bed with a new man, this takes the prize, she thinks, identifying animal poo in a country field. I can't wait to tell Becks about this.

'Not a wolf, I don't think,' she says to Dessi. 'Wolf poo would probably be bigger, more like dog poo.' She meets Cosmo's eyes brimming with laughter and says, 'Do you get a lot of wolves here, Dessi?'

'No, never, not a single one,' says Dessi sadly. 'But I hope one day we'll have one – wouldn't it be great? I've seen them on TV, and they look so lovely.'

'We're going for a walk in the forest – do you want

to come, Dessi?' Cosmo rises to his feet. 'You can decide which path.'

'OK, you two can follow me – I want to show Callista the dangerous dell.'

The dangerous dell, which seems very peaceful, is surrounded by large trees, and the path skirts the edge of the large and deep bowl-shaped depression where only grass grows.

'Is it dangerous to go down into it?' asks Callista when Dessi pauses to look down. 'Can we go down?'

'It's not dangerous now, but it was – a long time ago. Someone probably got eaten by a wolf or a bear down there. I'll hold your hand, if you like, if you feel scared.'

'It's surprising how much deeper it seems when you get down here.' Callista looks up to where they stood a couple of minutes ago. 'It must be thirty feet deep. How on earth do these things form? It's such an even shape, as if someone dug it out for a purpose – but who would have dug something so huge back in the days when they dug by hand? I presume it's old.'

'I don't know – Birdwood was the first house on this land that anyone can remember, so probably the forest was just used for timber before my ancestor bought it, but the dell has always been here, I think. My father collected old maps of the area and the dell is marked on them, right back to the oldest one from the seventeenth century. I'll show you later.'

Dessi clambers up the steep slope ahead of them and Cosmo says in a low voice, 'It's not officially called the dangerous dell, on the maps it's just called "the dell" but Dessi made up a story about it when she discovered alliteration last year. She made up a lot of new names, so I became Clever Cosmo, and my mother was Good Grandma - and the dell became the Dangerous Dell.'

The forest stretches much further than Callista had expected and wherever they go Dessi finds something to stop and look at or to show Callista.

'There are two paths,' she explains. 'And they're kind of like the letter X – I'll draw you a map of the forest, so you know where to go. But now we have to go and fix the swing, Cosmo. You said you would, you promised – and I know you have time today, you've finished talking to people on the phone.'

The swing hangs from a branch of an oak on the very edge of the forest, diagonally across the field from the hencoop. 'See – way up there?' Dessi stops beside it and points up. 'I saw it when I was swinging really high and looking straight up so I'd get dizzy. It might break!'

The rope is frayed halfway up with tufts of pale fibres sticking out of the weather-darkened rope.

'Let's go and get the ladder,' says Cosmo. 'There's some rope in the big shed and I think we should replace both sides so they're new at the same time.'

'If you don't need me, I'll go and call my mum and

275

change my jeans,' says Callista and studies her legs, soaked from her ankles to her knees from the expedition into the dell and muddy at the hems. 'But I'm very happy to stay if you think I can help.'

Cosmo looks at her legs and grins. 'You see why I told you not to bring any good clothes? Dessi and I are often wet and dirty. We'll be fine, we're used to doing things together. I'll go and get the ladder, Dessi.'

Halfway across the field he reaches out and takes Callista's hand and says casually, 'Will you marry me?'

It makes her smile. 'Of course, I'll marry you. What a romantic proposal, Cosmo – I hope it means you love me?'

'You know I do – I'll say it properly later,' he says and kisses her cold hand, and they both laugh and continue across the sloping meadow towards the house, and she looks up at it and thinks that living here will be like living in a haven, a place of peace and safety, and its relative remoteness feels like a bonus.

Chapter 29

B lessing the impulse that made her add her new jeans to the overnight bag in the last minute, Callista sits down on the little sofa in her bedroom and takes a deep breath before she calls her parents. She must talk to them and this is the perfect opportunity, while Dessi and Cosmo are busy with the swing and Mrs. St Clair is reading in the small sitting room. She feels nervous about this call, but she must do it today. There are so many things on her mind now, all connected to the anonymous letter, and she knows that sitting down to dinner with Cosmo and his mother and knowing about the connection to Anthony, without having told her parents what she has found out, would feel like a betrayal, like keeping them in the dark. She still doesn't know if Liz told her Dad about the letter, so there is the added complication of trying to guess

277

how he will react if he suddenly finds out that she knows. And she must explain about Cosmo and why she is here in his house, when her parents probably think of him as someone she should be wary of, or even dislike.

She Skypes her mother from her phone and then sits hesitating when Liz face pops up until she says, 'Has something happened, darling? Tell us, please – what's wrong?'

And Callista can't quite think of a good way of starting the conversation, but start she must, so she says, 'Did you tell Dad? About the letter? Sorry, I've got some news and I need to know first - did you?'

'Of course, I did! Don't worry about it - he's right here beside me.'

Half of her Dad's face appears beside Liz's and he says, 'Is that what you're in a state about? Please don't worry – I know I'm your Dad, even if I'm not your father.'

Callista feels a weight slide from her shoulders and smiles at her parents. 'No – yes, I mean - that's one thing. But you've got to both listen to quite a long story, if you have time?'

And she nearly giggles at the phrase while her mother looks increasingly worried. 'Of course, we have time - come on, tell us what is happening, please! I'm beginning to get nervous – you seem to be quite worked up about something.'

It takes a long time to relate the whole story. Her parents have never heard of the lift incident, and she is reluctant to mention it, so she skips that part and says that Cosmo offered to drive her back after the TV interview and that they stopped at Okehampton.

'Why?' exclaims her mother. 'What on earth made you go up there at night and you hardly know the man!'

And Callista sits there in her room in Birdwood House and realises that this is getting quite confusing, and she'd better get her story line sorted out fast. 'Let's back up a bit, Mum. I didn't mention some of the most important things – I'll go right back to when I first met Cosmo in the make-up room at the TV studio.'

From there she keeps it chronological; she describes the sensation she felt when she first met Cosmo's eyes in the mirror, the undefinable sensation she refers to as a force field, and how she could feel it flowing out towards her during the interview, and how she knew he was running interference to help her.

'So, when the lift stopped and I had a full-on claustrophobic panic attack, he sorted it. And then I ...'

'What!?' says her Dad. 'You got into a lift? I can't believe it - you never use lifts. And what do you mean, he sorted it? How the hell did he do that? We've never been able to. I didn't think anything could stop the panic until you were out of whatever closed space caused it - and even then, it usually took ages for you to calm down.'

'I know - it's so strange, Dad, but he did. He just took hold of me – we were sitting on the floor in the dark and I was a complete mess, I think the combination of the lights going out and being in such a small space, it totally freaked me out, worse than anything you've ever seen me do. I pushed my nails right into the palms of my hands and I was bleeding, but I didn't know that until later. He just pulled me over and held me really close and said all kinds of comforting things, a bit like you would to a child who's having a nightmare, nothing that made much sense at the time, and suddenly, very soon actually, I felt as if my bones had melted, and all the tension was gone and the fear – all that paralyzing terror that you've seen happen to me, and that awful feeling that I'm about to die – just gone! And then I fell asleep, nearly instantly and the poor guy sat there for an hour holding me while I slept. And then the lift started up and the lights came on and we left. And *then* we went to Okehampton.'

At the end of this long rambling story there is total silence for a moment from her parents' end and then her mother says calmly, 'And then you fell in love with him?'

Callista grins. 'I think I was in love with him before

the lift stopped at the ground floor – I just didn't understand it until later.'

After five minutes of questions and more or less coherent explanations, she gets to the crux of her call. 'So anyway, here I am.'

She gets up and standing in the middle of the room she turns slowly in a circle with her phone held out to show where she is. 'This is one of the bedrooms at Birdwood House, where I'm a guest of Cosmo's mother for the weekend – and his guest as well, of course, he lives here too.'

From there the story becomes easier to tell, about who Dessi is and why Cosmo is her guardian and from there she continues to how they looked at the photo album last night and how Louise told her about Virginia.

'So, Cosmo's mother was best friends with Anthony's younger sister, a few years younger than him by the look of them in the photos, maybe five or six. And the album has lots of pictures of them at her twenty-first party – she only showed me because she was so staggered by my likeness to Virginia, who's been dead for five decades and never had children. She thought I must be Anthony's child, that he got someone pregnant and left some girl to bring me up on her own, or perhaps she thought he had an affair with someone who was married. So, I told her he was the sperm donor, and I showed her the letter. She thinks Anthony's a bit crazy these days, but she hasn't seen him for years and she says I'm the spitting image of Virginia and I even wind my hair around my left forefinger the way she used to!'

'Cripes!' says her Dad. 'What an extraordinary coincidence!'

Her mother looks searchingly at her. 'Two things, darling – are you really and truly in love with him?'

And Callista replies with total conviction, 'Mum, I love him so much I get breathless even thinking about him! What's the second thing?'

'I hope Anthony doesn't make it public that you're his biological daughter – I really do! I think that would generate more interest than any of us can imagine, quite devastating for you.'

'I know, so do we all here. It would be ghastly. What do you think, Dad?'

'Oh, I don't think he will. Why would he do that now, all of sudden?' says her Dad reasonably. 'You've been in the news for a while now, and that letter hasn't been made public by whoever wrote it. When Liz showed me the photo of it, I thought right away that it reads like a private communication, no threat of so-called exposure or any malice. Well, not apart from that bit where he or she says something about you taking after Anthony who is a bit mad. And if he or she does make it public, we'll just say, "no comment" and cope with it. These things fade out of the news after a while, it wouldn't last forever.'

'No, they don't – you're so right, Dad. And here's another good thought provided by Louise – that's Cosmo's mother – she said if these things happen when I'm close to someone who's is about to kill someone else, then it's not statistically likely that I'll ever again be in that situation. And the fact that it's happened twice is astonishing. I've been thinking about it ever since she said it, and I think she's right. I probably walk past people on the street who think 'I'm so mad with her I could kill her' and all sorts of other things, but they don't actually mean in it, they're not about to commit some act of violence, but when it really *was* somebody's intent to kill someone and I was physically close to them, then my mind was invaded by their thoughts.'

'And how did Cosmo react to that idea? I imagine that is exactly what he thinks is impossible, isn't it? All those quotes of comments he made the last couple of weeks – a true sceptic. How will you two deal with being on different planets about this?' Callista's mother sounds serious now, her face reveals her concern that this is going to be a problem.

'Those quotes lately are things he said a couple of years ago in a different context, so don't worry.' She smiles at her parents. 'He has refused to comment since the Salcombe video came out – he's been asked several times, but he just says he has nothing further to add.

He will continue to debunk modern myths about crop circles and talk about geology and fracking when asked, but he's retired from having opinions about ESP.'

She leaves it open, because she is not about to say that Cosmo now believes that what happened to her is exactly what it seems, another person's thought appearing in her mind. That's something only he can do.

Text message to Becks: *Got engaged.*

From Becks: *Congratulations, must be that Cosmo guy, good choice. Did revenge sex clinch the deal?*

From Callista: *No, love sex did the trick. How did you guess it was Cosmo?*

From Beck: *Don't be daft. I'm not blind or deaf and not as stupid as I'm blond-looking.*

Chapter 30

THREE MONTHS LATER

Becks holds the nail varnish bottle up to the light and says, 'I'm never going to buy this brand again, I'm sure it's programmed to start getting gluggy when at least half of it is left, a total rip-off.' And then out of the blue she adds, 'But I've been going to tell you that the more I think about Louise's theory about why that crazy ESP thing happened to you, the more realistic it seems – more reasonable than anything else that anyone has come up with. Duds and I were talking about it the other day – not that it explains *how* you knew what those two guys were thinking, but that it only happened those two times. You've never had any other alien thoughts pop into your head, have you?'

'No, never - just those two thinking about actually killing someone.'

'Well, there you are then – the odds that it would ever happen more than twice to anyone in the universe is not worth thinking about. So, you can relax now – you've done your share of ESP. *Have* you relaxed about it?'

'I have – well, not completely, but I'm working on it. I tell myself at least once a week that Louise's explanation is rational and credible. I probably won't relax completely until nothing like it has happened again for years. And it was also true that the media attention would wind down after a while, as everyone predicted. The media aren't interested in me now, thank goodness, and I get no funny parcels or weird messages. Bliss!'

Taking the bottle out of Becks' hand she says, 'Let me deal with that for you,' and disappears into the bathroom, leaving Becks staring after her and shaking her head. 'If you're thinking of throwing it in the bin, please don't! I've managed to do one hand and I want to do the other one before I toss it.'

Callista comes back shaking the bottle and hands it to Becks. 'I've fixed it - I wasn't going to throw it in the bin. I just poured a couple of drops of nail varnish remover in it to dilute it a bit. Let me know when your nails are dry enough, and we'll go out and have lunch somewhere nice. Since I moved out, I haven't seen anywhere near enough of you outside the staffroom at school. Or is Dudley expected back for lunch?'

'No, they're all having lunch together, Saturday rehearsals sometimes go on until mid-afternoon if there's no early wedding – that choir is his second family. And you could see more of me quite easily, you know. Birdwood House is only – what? – fifteen or twenty miles from town. When is Cosmo coming back?'

'Tuesday evening. Dessi has spent days dusting the model railway in the attic – she and Joan were planning to move some of the old furniture around up there and make it more like a "railway sitting room" - she told me this morning, when I asked if she wanted to come. She said she wants it all finished and nice for when Cosmo comes home. I think we're going to spend a lot of time in the attic now the trains are working again.'

'She's called Titslinger? What an extraordinary name,' says Becks an hour later and starts laughing. 'You're having me on, aren't you? She's called Brown or Smith or something. You made it up!'

'Well, she's actually called Titzinger, but Dessi got it wrong when she heard us talking about it a couple of weeks ago, so now we're all going to have to be really careful that we get it right if we mention her to people.'

'Ah, she's probably used to it,' says Becks unfeelingly and turns to reach for the sugar straws on the table behind them. 'And why is she doing the catering anyway? I thought Joan One and Joan Two would do it.

'Heavens, no! They are wedding guests – the older Joan has booked an appointment for a manicure, would you believe, for the first time ever. And I can't wait to see what the younger Joan is going to wear – she's into mid-century clothes in a big way, belongs to the rock-and-roll club and wears dresses with full skirts and starched petticoats. Louise has invited everyone who works at Birdwood House, including Adele who cleans and the two guys who do the garden – she says she thought Cosmo would never find anyone he could be serious about, so it must be celebrated properly, everyone must be invited.'

'And what is Dessi wearing? Something a bit like my dress – like a child version?'

'No, she's wearing her daffodil dress, which is yellow, of course – her second favourite colour after red. And the hat.'

'The hat?'

'Sorry, I didn't explain it very well. It's an outfit Cosmo bought her for a fancy-dress party with a head-dress shaped like a daffodil flower and a matching dress - both look as if they're made from yellow petals, and green tights - like stalks. She is currently deciding if she should have new shoes or just wear her red sneakers.'

'Really? Or are you kidding?'

'Oh, no – why wouldn't we let her? She loves the dress, and it's really cute and when we said she could be the flower girl, she straight away said "and I've already got a flower dress, isn't that great" so we decided she could wear it. Louise thinks we're a bit mad, but it will make a fabulous wedding photo and when she's a teenager she'll probably forbid us to show it to anyone. Cosmo says he'll have it printed – large and in colour and present it to her as a twenty-first birthday card.'

Becks stirs her coffee and says casually, 'What a lucky child she is to have parents like you two! I tried on my lovely bridesmaid's dress last night – I must have put on a bit of weight, it's a tiny bit tight, so I'd better watch what I eat this week.'

Then she opens her mouth in an O and stares into space for a moment and Callista starts laughing. 'Becks, didn't you know you're pregnant?'

And Becks looks as if she is in a dream and says slowly, 'Good God, I must be – I had no idea, how the hell did that happen? Did *you* know?'

'I thought you must be, and I've been waiting for you to tell me. Are you OK?'

'I think so – I don't feel upset, I'm just surprised. And Duds will be happy – that was one of the things that made him so cute and endearing that day when I first ran into him in Cathedral Close. We were walking up the hill together talking about this and that - and I asked him what he wanted most from the future – it was rather an odd conversation to have with someone you've only just met, now that I think about it – and he said, "I want to be a father while I'm still young and can enjoy doing lots of things with my kids". I think I fell in love with him on the spot. And I'm twenty-nine, so I've got to get started some time.'

'Thank God it's a warm day!' says Liz one week later and holds the car door open for Callista to get in before she hands her the flowers. 'I just got a text from Cosmo - Dessi and Becks are in Dudley's car and should be at St Mary's in about fifteen minutes and they'll wait for us in the vestibule. So, let's go and get you married!'

When they turn from the altar after taking their vows, everyone gets to their feet and Cosmo and Callista walk down the aisle, not arm in arm as most couples do, but hand in hand, followed by Dessi and Becks also hand in hand. And Callista notices a man standing alone in the last pew on her side. Their eyes meet and she recognizes his face from the photos she found on the Internet a few months ago. She smiles and he smiles back, and then they are outside on the church steps and family and friends, who have followed them out, surround them with congratulations and hugs. When she looks around some minutes later he has gone, but she smiles at the thought that she has exchanged a smile with her biological father.

Many Thanks

We hope you've enjoyed reading this story and would consider leaving a review on your favourite review site, or with the retailer you purchased from.

These are not only much appreciated, they also help other readers discover new authors.

For more in this ongoing series, plus other titles, please read on.

Letters from the Past

Letters from the Past is a series of stand-alone novels where a letter from or about the past reveals something that changes a woman's perceptions of herself or of her family, and that affects her outlook on life.

These books are such fun to write, and I am always working on the next title in this series. I hope you will enjoy reading them as much as I enjoy writing them!

Tina

LARA'S HOUSE

TINA CLOUGH

LETTERS FROM THE PAST SERIES

Having had nobody in her life since her husband died, Lara unexpectedly finds herself involved with three men. One is planning to use her, one she plans to use for her own ends, and one becomes a "friend-with-benefits" with surprising results. Sometimes a quiet schoolteacher is not all she seems at first glance.

Callista experiences an event of apparent ESP at the Okehampton Castle ruins and becomes a media sensation, but the effect it has on her life is dramatic. How do two people, one calm. one seriously claustrophobic, who feel they are poles apart, cope for an hour and a half in total darkness in a stalled lift? And can they handle the consequences?

Sofia's life is in turmoil: a difficult diva mother, a letter with a confession about a family killing and having to accept help from a man she loathes when she is injured. Can reluctant attraction turn into love?

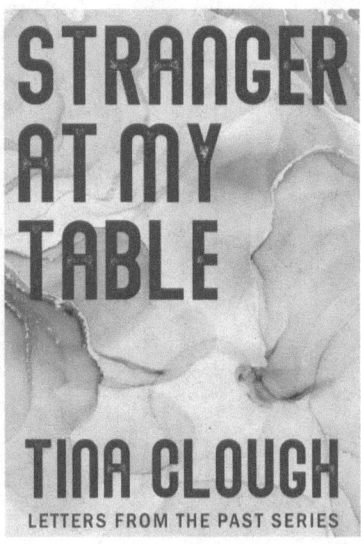

STRANGER AT MY TABLE

TINA CLOUGH

LETTERS FROM THE PAST SERIES

Who is the stranger living in the empty house Miranda inherited from her grandmother? Why is he living like a secretive recluse in someone else's house? Reckless Miranda decides to confront him, and what she discovers prompts her to set out on a fearless quest to bring justice to a man who has given up hope. But is the gamble too great or a risk worth taking?

DEEP WATER

TINA CLOUGH

LETTERS FROM THE PAST SERIES

When Emma finds an old letter in a library book she is instantly intrigued, but by researching the origin of the letter she unwittingly opens the door to danger and becomes the target for threats and harassment. Nearly desperate, she takes a leap of blind faith into the unknown and accepts an offer of help from a stranger - but can she trust him?

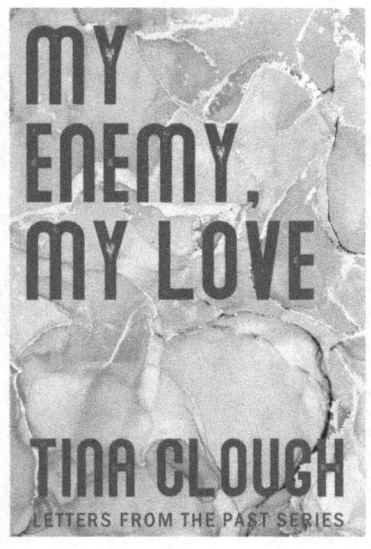

MY ENEMY, MY LOVE

TINA CLOUGH

LETTERS FROM THE PAST SERIES

Jamie, an ardent protester against the gigantic Vista Resort development and Leo Masters, the high-powered developer, seem unlikely to ever agree on anything. But unexpected coincidences and chance brings them together in a fragile state of mutual respect. Will courage and kindness resolve the situation, or do they need help?

After a bizarre accident with ESP overtones, the media haunt Arapera. But can she trust an offer of help from a man she has only met once? Or will she regret it for the rest of her life if she doesn't take the chance? Sometimes life is a knife-edge balance between staying safe and taking risks, and there is no way of predicting if the gamble is worth it.

Also by Tina Clough

THE GIRL WHO LIVED TWICE

What would you do if you woke up one morning and found that time had rewound exactly a year? Would you revisit your past mistakes and try to do better? Would you try to get revenge on those who had wronged you? Or would you use what you knew to get rich? When Mia finds herself in her own past, she must decide how best to use her pre-knowledge of one year's worth of events and personal issues.

303

RUNNING TOWARDS DANGER

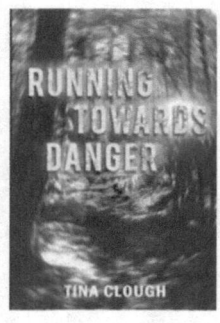

When Karen's flat-mate Nick is gunned down in front of her in the street her life is turned upside-down. Everything she thought she knew about him turns out to be a lie. She becomes a suspect in the police investigation and drug bosses think she knows where Nick has hidden a large sum of money. When her life is threatened, she decides to leave town and disappear.

Karen becomes Cara and creates an anonymous existence, severs all links to her past and adopts a cash-based way of life that leaves no electronic traces. But despite her careful planning danger still stalks her and she is forced to make dramatic choices in the face of threats and brutal violence.

Can she trust the man she is attracted to, or has he been sent by the killers to gain her confidence and find the money they believe she has?

THE CHINESE PROVERB

Book 1 - Hunter Grant Series

Army veteran Hunter Grant thought he had left war behind in Afghanistan – a conflict that left him with physical and psychological scars.

But finding an unconscious girl in the Northland bush and gradually untangling her story involves him in warfare of a different kind in his own country.

Hunter sets out to find and punish the man Dao calls Master, but he soon finds there is more to this story than enslavement. Before long he himself is being hunted by the overlord of a drug empire whose sole objective is to kill Dao because she knows too much.

Protecting her and waging war while trying to keep the police from stifling his enterprise takes all Hunter's ingenuity and determination and puts him in deadly jeopardy.

ONE SINGLE THING

Book 2 - Hunter Grant Series

Journalist Hope Barber disappears two weeks after returning to New Zealand from an assignment in Pakistan, leaving her front door open and her bag and phone inside. The police are tight-lipped about their reluctance to act, and Hunter Grant and Dao agree to help Hope's brother Noah find her. Details about Hope's time in Pakistan gradually emerge but only raise more questions.

Was Hope under surveillance?

Was she linked to terrorists?

And who is the man Hope called 'my stalker'?

FOLDED

Book 3 - Hunter Grant Series

First notes asking for help and folded into tiny origami shapes are found outside a city apartment building, then a physics textbook with tiny writing between the lines and then the woman who found them abruptly resigns and disappears. Are the notes asking for help real or is it a game? Hunter Grant, ex-army and with a pragmatic view of justice, reluctantly agrees to help find the missing woman.

Things get complicated when a high-powered lawyer arrives form the US, and shortly after his meeting with Hunter and Dao, a "cease and desist" letter arrives from the Cayman Islands. Inspector Bakker - a woman, who in Hunter's words "looks as if she would be useful in a brawl, provided she was on your side" - takes instant exception to his involvement and threatens to arrest him for interfering in an investigation.

Dao sets out alone on a dangerous mission, driven by a compulsive need to find out what has happened to the girl who wrote the notes, and Hunter looks death in the face when he decides to risk everything to put an end to the Darknet forces that threaten their lives.

THE SHADOW BROKER

It is 2026 and individual freedoms are severely curtailed, with state surveillance everywhere. State Security has a Watch List, and being on it means that nothing you do or say escapes the authorities, but does the Kill List really exist? And if it does, how would you know if you were on it?

Coded messages on a found burner phone, top-level government corruption and a shadowy mastermind who calls himself The Broker. In this climate of state control, three unlikely friends start quietly looking for connections and set in motion a deadly game of hide and seek that will change their lives forever.

Trying to uncover the truth means risking your life, and nothing is more dangerous than searching for evidence of government corruption.

About the Author

Tina Clough grew up in Sweden and now lives in New Zealand; dividing her time between writing fiction and translating and editing medical research papers.

Between working and writing she looks after an acre of fruit trees, vegetable gardens and roaming hens.

Apart from reading her interests include photography, wine, growing organic vegetables, making jam and kayaking.

https://lightpoolpublishing.com

PRAISE FOR BILL PRYST

"Bill Pryst... the greatest literary talent of... the twenty first century... hands down." - The East Shoshone Journal of Excellence.

"I don't have to know him to hate him." - John Remy

"In two weeks I'll be 99.9% certain if he's the father of my child." - Beatrice Smothers

"Bill Pryst is one of the finest crochet artists I've ever seen" - Margaret Lee

"After reading this heart warming... action packed... romance... I now know the true meaning of horror." - Southern Baptist School for Scientology

"I read this book to my child as a bedtime story and I'm proud to say they're releasing him from county in just two weeks." - Maria Heartgrove

"It could have been the shellfish, but after reading Bill's book I had the best night of sex ever, and then puked all morning." - Brian Lasange

"If I had a choice between reading this again or going down on a goat, I'd have to really think about it." - Ronald Cohen

"When was the last time you boom-boomed your wife? This book will give you a reason to do it again." - Tom Lawrence of Bam-Bam Monthly

PRAISE FOR BILL PRYST

"I bought a large print copy, so I could tape it outside my shower." - Blind Mike

"I had to call a doctor because my erection lasted over four hours." - Sam Brownstone

"In Muslim nations, this book is forced to wear a veil." - Ahmad Talami Tirik Husseini

"My warts haven't been back in months." - Butch Tempor

"Don't buy this piece of trash unless you're out of shit paper." - Tim Buruck

"I've been crippled since birth. Last week I ran the New York Marathon. Thank you Bill Pryst!" - Denise Gould

"Just because I licked coke off his balls, doesn't mean I like the guy." - Tina Rodriguez

"I used to be a heterosexual male. After reading Bill's book, straight up the ass for me, all day long." - Mike Billings

"Would I fuck this book? My dog hasn't eaten peanut butter in months. Does that answer your question?" - Reggie Asante

"It was like reading my five year old's journal, except the cover didn't have a stick figure drawn on it." - Bryce Stevens

"Mr. Pryst inspired me to go back into the closet." - Richard Brenner

MORE PRAISE FOR BILL PRYST

"After reading this book, I stopped believing in God" - Jesus Christ

"To keep it real, Bill wrote his own unauthorized biography." - You Weekly

"*Bill Pryst* is French slang for rectal bleeding." - Françoise

"I refuse to believe in the type of God that would make Bill Pryst, and watch him prosper." - Franklin Belaire - Foundation of Atheist Glorification

"This book was so bad it made me punch my wife. And this time, she didn't deserve it." - Gregg Lifano

"My dog ate my copy, I never read it. Why, is it good?" - Bill Pryst

"I made a suit out of the pages because I wanted his words all over me." - Jane Peck

"...of the more controversial items found in Osama bin Laden's compound: a naked picture of Bill Pryst..." - Mary Stevenson-Smith - Associated News

"Holy fucking average!" - Roger Hart

"I'll tell you how much I liked it: shredded, burned, buried." - Elisabeth Rowly

"I don't know about the book, but Bill Pryst is sexy!" - Art the Trucker

MORE PRAISE FOR BILL PRYST

"I'm not saying he's not talented. I'm just saying Hitler was talented, too." - Professor Brown Browning - Brown University

"I scream Bill Pryst's name when I masturbate. You should, too." - Samantha Renaldo

"God may have been part of the train they ran on Bill's mom that night. No mortal could write this good." - Tempest Book Review

"I left my children to Bill in my will." - Thomas Monroe

"I am officially one of the eight idiots who have read this drivel." - Martin Ballard

"It was like having a stranger piss in my mouth. So, yeah, I enjoyed it." - Christina Tanningdale

"I used the audio version so my hands were free to roam while I listened." - Clarissa Stevenson

"My son said he wanted to be Bill Pryst for Halloween. I had no idea that meant he'd be attending an orgy." - Mrs. Laura Polack

"I have a life-sized cardboard cut-out of him in my room with a cucumber glued to it... for the lonely nights." - Kate Brooks

"Incest is best, put your sister to the test. That's what I always say. Seriously, I say it all the time." - Mark Phantom – President Bill Pryst Fan Club

EVEN MORE PRAISE FOR BILL PRYST

"When I think of Bill Pryst, as I often do, I think of him as Zeus in human form, on earth to bed underage maidens. I hope that helps." - Brandt Solomon, Professor of Literature, Princeton

"This book single handedly saved one thousand Jews from the holocaust." - Hanz Schreiber, Auschwitz

"NASA has announced that it will begin carving a life size replica of Bill Pryst's penis into the surface of the moon. The eight billion dollar, government funded project, will take approximately three years to complete. Unfortunately, due to the limited surface area of the moon, only 60% will be visible at any given time." - Press Secretary, Bob Givens.

"If I had a nickel for every cat I've fucked, I'd be a rich man. Huh? Oh yeah, the book, top notch." - Richard Tumor

"I learned far more from this book than I ever did in school. No, I didn't read it, I can't read. But I'm sure it's good." - Stan Thomas

"More exciting than a bubble bath with bisexual twins on ecstasy." - North San Juan Mall Review

"I wrap my husband's member with the pages before we make love. As of today we're expecting our tenth set of twins." - Shirley Baker

"…with a style as smooth as an epileptic off his meds…." - Rotten Eggs Starred Review

MORE AND MORE PRAISE FOR BILL PRYST

"It might be irresponsible to say that Mr. Pryst's writings cure cervical cancer, but I'm saying it anyway." - Dr. John Mersing, MD

"Don't look at me. I wanted her to have an abortion." - Walt Pryst

"It made my pussy sigh." - Nora Briggs, Happy Willow Retirement Home

"I swear to God dude, the entire gerbil, up the ass." - Steven White

"It puts the 'Oh shit, my wife's home' back into sex." - Reginald Jones

"After reading Mr. Pryst's book, my penis has grown two inches and my stamina has never been better. Thanks Bill!" - Larry & Beth Sanchez

"It's like getting your tubes tied without anesthetic." - Worldly Globe

"Bill gave me the crabs." - Jill Simpson

"Twice." - Silvia Cornerstone

"And it was worth it." - Sarah Elovia

"I never thought of a horse as a sexual being, then I read Bill's book. Now I live on a farm in West Virginia…" - Torrance Brown